Belieber!

FAME, FAITH, AND THE HEART OF
JUSTIN BIEBER

CATHLEEN FALSANI

Copyright © 2011 by Cathleen Falsani

Published by Worthy Publishing, a division of Worthy Media, Inc., 134 Franklin Road, Suite 200, Brentwood, Tennessee 37027.

HELPING PEOPLE EXPERIENCE THE HEART OF GOD

eBook available at www.worthypublishing.com

Audio distributed through Oasis Audio; visit www.oasisaudio.com

Library of Congress Control Number: 2011936271

Scripture quotations in this book are taken from *The Message*. Copyright © 1993, 1994, 1995, 1996, 2000, 2001, 2002. Used by per mission of NavPress Publishing Group.

For foreign and subsidiary rights, contact Riggins International Rights Services, Inc.; www.rigginsrights.com

Published in association with Yates & Yates, LLP, www.yates2.com

ISBN: 978-1-936034-77-2 (trade paperback)

Cover Design: FaceOut Studio
Cover Photo: Steve Thorne/Getty Images
Interior Design: FaceOut Studio
Interior photos: Courtesy of the *Toronto Star* ©2011, except for photo 108931148 (RM) *Justin Beiber: Never Say Never* Los Angeles Premiere—Red Carpet, Todd Williamson/ Wire Image/Getty Images
Photo Insert Design: Richmond & Williams, Brentwood, TN
Typesetting: Kristi Smith, Juicebox Designs

Printed in the United States of America

11 12 13 14 15 RRD 8 7 6 5 4 3 2 1

For Uncle Veen—
With love and squalor

Contents

Giving Back

Save one life and you save the world entire.
— THE TALMUD, SANHEDRIN 37A

In keeping with Justin's commitment to "pay it forward," a portion of the proceeds from the sale of *Belieber!: Fame, Faith, and the Heart of Justin Bieber* will be donated to the Global Fund to Fight AIDS, Tuberculosis, and Malaria. For more information about the Global Fund and other ways you can take action, please visit www.theglobalfund.org.

Note to Readers

Unless otherwise noted, all Scripture quotations are taken from *The Message*, Eugene Peterson's 2002 biblical "para-translation," which employs contemporary idioms that keep the original languages of the Bible "fresh, contemporary and understandable."

A few names have been changed in this book to protect the privacy of the individuals involved, and some of the direct quotes have been gently edited for clarity. Whenever possible, the direct quotes that appear in this book were taken from video and audio interviews with the speakers, or from first-person and/or authorized written accounts.

Chapter 1

Beliebing:
An Introduction

Every generation throws a hero up the pop charts.
— PAUL SIMON, "THE BOY IN THE BUBBLE"

Don't let anyone put you down because you're young.
Teach believers with your life: by word, by demeanor,
by love, by faith, by integrity.
— 1 TIMOTHY 4:12

SCENE 1

The place:
Senior High Sunday school room
Basement level, North Park Baptist Church
Bridgeport, Connecticut

The time:
Mid-morning on a Sunday
Early August 1985

The players:
Your author, age 15, and a dozen other high school students

The setting:
The Sunday school teacher asks if there are any prayer requests

1

Should I? They'll think I'm stupid. They'll probably laugh at me. David will say something snotty to make fun of me. He's always quick to make me look like a dork if he can. (Probably because he likes me and won't admit it.) But . . . the guys really need our prayers. Oh, what the heck . . .

I raise my hand.

"Yes, Cathi," Rex, the Sunday school teacher, says and nods in my direction.

He'll get it. Rex used to be a rock-'n'-roll guy before he got saved. A roadie, I think. What was the band again? Twisted Sister? Meatloaf?

"Yeah, um . . . I think we really should pray for the members of the band U2," I say, tentatively.

A few people giggle. A few more stare at me like I'm crazy.

"Because, well, I know this guy at my school who has friends in Boston, and they're, like, friends of the band," I continue, trying to ignore the giggling. "And there's this old couple there who are friends with Bono and have prayed for him for years and stuff. He calls them 'Ma and Pa,' or something like that. Anyway, so you know how U2 are Christians? . . ."

Full-on laughter interrupts me for a moment.

"They are! Seriously!" I say, raising my voice a little, which shuts them up. David stops laughing, looks like he's going to say something mean, but then seems to change his mind, sweeping his long bangs out of his eyes and staring glumly at his spotless Air Jordans.

I'm starting to blush, from aggravation, not embarrassment.

"Go ahead, Cathi," Rex urges.

"They totally are Christians. Well, at least Bono and The Edge and Larry are. Adam isn't, I guess, but still," I continue, the pounding in my chest slowing and my hot cheeks beginning to cool. "So Bono was talking to this couple recently, and he asked them to pray for him and the band because he thinks they're on the verge of becoming huge, especially after Live Aid. He said he's worried about being super-famous and that it might bring a lot of pressure to not be Christians. He's worried about how fame might change them or affect their faith. So I thought we should pray for them, that God would be close to them especially right now and protect them and guard their hearts."

And then we prayed.

We prayed for the members of U2 to be strong in their faith. We prayed for the bass player, Adam Clayton, to become a Christian. We prayed for the band's protection while they travel, for God to surround them with good people who would support them in their faith. We thanked God for placing "believers," as we called them, in a position where they could influence people positively in a unique way. We prayed that God would use U2 and their music to reach more people with God's love.

Even though I ran the risk of looking like a total band geek, I'm glad I spoke up. A few weekends before that Sunday, my alarm clock sounded before sunrise. I wrestled myself from sleep and tiptoed downstairs in my pajamas. I switched on the television, tuned it to MTV, and turned the volume way down so I wouldn't awaken my parents or my little brother whose bedrooms were nearby. Rubbing sleep from my eyes, I found the remote stuck between two cushions of the couch, grabbed a throw blanket, and settled into the not-so-comfortable chair closest to the TV set.

At the time, my family didn't own a VCR and this was a good twenty years before digital video recorders were invented, so if I wanted to watch Live Aid, the huge benefit concert in London—and, simultaneously, in Philadelphia—organized by Irish rocker Bob Geldof to raise money for Africans suffering through a terrible famine in Ethiopia, I had to get up in the dark and watch it live. In 1985, the Internet wasn't even a pixilated glimmer in anyone's imagination, so there were no websites listing who was performing when, no video streaming online, and no YouTube to watch clips later. If I didn't want to miss my favorite band play during the concert at London's Wembley Stadium, my only choice was to watch from the very beginning, just to be sure.

By the time I got settled in my chair in the living room, it was almost noon in London, where the Live Aid concert was about to begin, and I had a fierce case of what I call "crawly butt"—that mixture of pins-and-needles jumpiness and a vague kind of sweaty nausea you get when you can't wait for something to happen. Images from Wembley filled the television screen. A British military band took the stage and played the British national anthem, "God Save the Queen," followed by two bands I'd never heard of: Status Quo and Style Council. About twenty minutes into the live broadcast from London, the first act with a name that I recognized hit the stage: The Boomtown Rats. This was Geldof's band, the guy who organized Live Aid and, the Christmas before, the Band Aid album with two dozen rock-'n'-roll stars from England and Ireland, including members of Duran Duran, The Police, and U2.

For the next five hours, I didn't move, except for occasional potty breaks between sets. Finally, shortly after 10 a.m., in the neatly appointed Connecticut home where I grew up, surrounded by artwork and memorabilia from my parents' many world travels, U2 walked onto the stage at Wembley. I burst into tears, turning the volume up to ear-ringing levels (the rest of my family had gone out for the day) and hanging on every word Bono uttered.

It was an epic performance–one that, many years later, is credited as the turning point in U2's storied career, thrusting them out of mere popularity into superstardom. U2 opened with their song "Sunday Bloody Sunday" and then launched into a nearly thirteen-minute-long version of "Bad."

"Isolation, Desolation, let it go! . . . I'm wide awake! I'm not sleepin' . . ." Bono howled, passion rising in his face like the Irish flush that reddened his cheeks.

Clad in black like a sprightly Johnny Cash, Bono whooped, strutted, and marched around the stage. Lifting his hands in the air and crouching down as if in prayer, the twenty-five-year-old front man tossed his (admittedly ill-conceived in retrospect) dyed-black, frosted-tipped mullet like a pony, owning every inch of the enormous outdoor stage. Midway through the song, he dropped his microphone with a resounding thud and climbed onto a low riser between the main stage and the vast crowd pushing its way toward the barricades at the front of the stadium. Waving his hands above his head and gesticulating toward the crowd, Bono motioned for security to help several young women being crushed by the weight of the crowd behind them over the barricades. When that didn't happen fast enough, Bono leapt down to the audience level, helped pull a few girls from the throng of fans, grabbed one lucky lady in a tight hug, and then slow-danced with her.

I swooned, positively beside myself with envy.

After hugging and chastely kissing a few other girls who also had been rescued from the thousands-strong mass of humanity pressing to get as close to the Irish rocker as it could, Bono returned to the stage and finished the song. Before exiting stage left, he grabbed a white towel to wipe the sweat from his brow, twirled it like a flag, and spoke to the audience one last time. "GOD BLESS YOU!" he shouted.

Again I dissolved into joyful tears, thrilled to my bones about what I had just witnessed. It was so moving, so visceral, and he even mentioned God! I had been a fan of U2 for several years by the time the band played Live Aid on July 13, 1985, but I had only ever listened to their albums or heard their music on the radio. I'd never watched them perform. In fact, it would be another twenty years before I finally saw them play live in person. (When I was in high school, my parents forbade me from attending rock concerts lest I begin to fall down some slippery slope. And when I was in college and graduate school, I couldn't afford the price of admission.)

Still, as a teenager I bragged about having been a U2 fan "from the very beginning," when they released their first album, *Boy*, in 1980. I had all of their albums and cared for them as if they were precious jewels. Posters and pictures of the band purchased at the mall record store or torn from magazines—particularly shots of Bono, with whom I was completely infatuated—covered the walls of my bedroom. I devoured even the tiniest bit of news that I could find in the newspapers about the Irish rockers. Being half-Irish and a young Christian unapologetically obsessed with music (but cautioned by well-meaning youth pastors that rock-'n'-roll surely was "of the devil"), I felt a unique kind of kinship with the band. I knew their story—how they grew up in a working-class part of Dublin during years of violent clashes between Catholics and Protestants in Ireland that my parents called "the Troubles"; how Bono, The Edge, Larry Mullen Jr., and Adam Clayton met while students at Mount Temple Comprehensive School in Dublin, the first school in Ireland where Catholic and Protestant children learned side by side; how Bono's mother, Iris, a Protestant, died suddenly when he was fourteen, and how Bono and his older brother, Norman, were raised through his

6

teen years by his father, Bob, a Catholic; how the band formed when they were just fifteen and sixteen years old; and how Bono, The Edge, and Larry attended an nondenominational church in Dublin called Shalom whose members would eventually question whether the boys could be both authentically Christian and secular rock musicians. Their story resonated with me deeply.

U2 was a godsend. Literally. Their music—the sound and the lyrics—inspired me, enlivened my burgeoning faith, and truly opened my heart to the Holy Spirit in profound ways that stay with me to this day. They sang songs about relationships—with God, family, parents, and friends—and falling in and out of love, about politics, war, peace, and their heroes, such as Martin Luther King Jr., whom they memorialized in their famous song, "Pride (In the Name of Love)." But they also sang about faith, doubt, and spiritual connection—the same ideas I heard in church and the Christian prep school I attended, but in a different way. It was honest, genuine, sometimes difficult, and it felt so real to me, as if they found the words for thoughts I wasn't brave enough (yet) to express out loud. "Oh Lord, loosen my lips . . ."

I first learned of the hardships and injustices faced by poor Africans through the band's involvement with Live Aid and continued to be educated about poverty, environmental concerns, political injustices around the world, the AIDS emergency in sub-Saharan Africa, and issues of faith and economics through their lyrics and Bono's activism as a rock star-diplomat tirelessly advocating for the "least of these" among us. Bono's outspoken challenge to express our faith not only in words but also in action challenged my notions of what it meant to be a true believer. He made me want to be a better person, give back, and do what I could to help heal the world.

Now at age forty, I am the mother of an African child who

was an AIDS orphan born into extreme poverty in Malawi (a tiny, bean-shaped country tucked between Zambia, Tanzania, and Mozambique). My son, Vasco, who is almost twelve years old, is himself a huge U2 fan (and a Belieber, though he'd crown me for saying so in public). As soon as he learned enough English to understand them, he quickly memorized the lyrics to the band's biblically themed songs, "Salome" and "Mysterious Ways." For months Vasco would awaken me each morning singing, "Shake, shake, shake SALOME!" and "She moves, she moves in mysterious ways!" at the top of his lungs. Were it not for the influence U2's music and personal endeavors in social justice had on me as a teenager, I honestly don't believe my life would have crossed paths with Vasco's and that we'd be a family today. The band had and continues to have a formative influence on my faith, life, and the way I see the world. And it all took root when I was just a kid—an emotional, terribly earnest fifteen-year-old infatuated with a newly popular rock band.

When I was in junior high and high school, my parents had misgivings about my passion for U2, although the fact that most of the band members were people of faith who often sang about their relationship with and love for God seemed to allay some of their concerns. Today my parents look back on their over-tired, pajama-clad, weepy teenage daughter glued to the television for hours and recognize that God was doing something in her heart all those years ago. A seed was planted that grew into something more beautiful, powerful, and grace-filled than any of us could have imagined.

It is easy for adults to dismiss the passions of teenagers as silly, frivolous, and fleeting. Teens and tweens can be mercurial, fickle, impulsive, hyper-emotional, given to whims and flights of fancy, jealously guarding obsessions they feel are positively essential one day only to abandon them the next. I once heard a comedian say that all children are fundamentalists. Their young hearts wholeheartedly believe whatever it is they believe, and despite any and all evidence to the contrary, they remain unmoved. For most children, things are good or bad, black or white, ugly or beautiful. They live in absolutes. Kids are, by nature, deeply faithful, even or perhaps especially when others (i.e., grownups) tell them they're wrong, too young to know better (or to be taken seriously), or just plain ridiculous.

Parents would do well to pay close attention to their children's passions. Some indeed may be short-lived, but others are indicative of the orientation of a child's heart and mind, a trajectory that could last a lifetime. Although, as the Bible says, there comes a time in everyone's lives to put away childish things, some artifacts of childhood remain, for better or for worse. The masterful Christian writer Frederick Buechner cautions all of us—young, old, and in-between—to "listen" to our lives. Pay attention to the things that bring a tear to your eye or a lump in your throat, he says, because "if you pay attention to those moments, you realize that something deep beneath the surface of who you are, something deep beneath the surface of the world, is trying to speak to you about who you are."

Sometimes listening to your life means taking careful notice of the music that moves your soul. Which brings me to the subject of this book—young Master Justin Drew Bieber of Stratford, Ontario, Canada.

SCENE 2

The place:
> My home office
> Laguna Beach, California

The time:
> Early on a Tuesday morning
> Mid-April 2011

The players:
> Your author, age 40, and some of the 9 million+ other people
> following Justin Bieber on Twitter at the time

The setting:
> Sitting in front of my computer, browsing through emails, Facebook
> status updates, and my Twitter feed, which is exploding with activity

Uh-oh. Something's up with Justin.

Tweet after tweet from across the planet arrived rapid-fire in the Twitter feed for people I was following, many of them devoted fans, or "Beliebers," as they are often called, of Mr. Bieber, the about-to-turn-seventeen-year-old musical superstar plucked from obscurity in his native Canada only a couple of years earlier.

A chorus of impassioned tweets scrolled across my computer screen—in a litany of outrage, emotional support, and prayers—140 characters at a time.

@Viicky_Belieber	#cheerupjustin ♥ the fans are here for you!! Te amamos <3 #muchlove
@laurenluvsnina	Dear paps, Please leave @justinbieber while he is in CHURCH!!!! In the place of God! Let him be in peace! Let him b able to *pray* in peace!

@xoivolina	@justinbieber read this and please #cheerupjustin !WE LOVE YOU!<3
@purpleglasses89	@justinbieber sorry youre not having the best experience in *Israel*, were all here for you! #muchlove #cheerupjustin
@Courtlillian	@justinbieber I'm SO sorry about the Paps!! I hope you're having the time of your life! Be strong, Pray and God will be with you, always :)
@BelieblnBiebz	@Justinbieber #cheerupjustin we all love & support u. I kno the *paps* are stupid but jus remember y u started doing this. #belieberlove <3
@just_sophi	Hey @justinbieber i berry sory that the paps are like thiis dont worry!! Just enjoy the moment with family,And pray ILOVEU and all your fans
@xoliviadancesx	#cheerupjustin your fans love & support you, it's disgusting how @justinbieber can't get any privacy. he's a person. BACK OFF PAPS!
@emilylamblv	@justinbieber I love u so much your so cute and don't worry about the paps god is with all the way ok so pray and plz tweet me back luv u

And on it went. For hours. Tweets from at least four continents and in a dozen languages. All leaping to Justin's defense. The Belieber Army was on high alert, mustering for possible retaliatory strikes.

What in the world happened? Was Justin hurt? And where was Justin's bodyguard, Kenny? He's never more than a few feet away from his young charge. I hope Justin's okay . . .

Because in 2011, the Twitterverse moves faster than the twenty-four-hour online news cycle and light-years ahead of TV news, I clicked over to Justin's official Twitter feed and scrolled down hoping to figure out what had gone down.

Scroll. Scroll. Scroll. Aha!

There it was: angry dispatches hastily typed by the lad himself in the middle of the night.

Beginning at 3:16 a.m. in Tel Aviv, Israel (where he was preparing to perform in concert two days later), Justin posted a series of tweets that he later described as "frustrated."

@justinbieber, April 12, 2011

> You would think paparazzi would have some respect in holy places. All I wanted was the chance to walk where jesus did here in israel.

> They should be ashamed of themselves. Take pictures of me eating but not in a place of prayer, ridiculous

> People wait their whole lives for opportunities like this, why would they want to take that experience away from someone

> Staying in the hotel for the rest of the week u happy?

What went down earlier in the day, apparently, was this:

Justin, along with his parents, Pattie Mallette and Jeremy Bieber, manager Scooter Braun, and other friends, traveled north of Tel Aviv to visit the Church of the Multiplication in the town of Tabgha, Israel. The church is said to mark the location where Jesus performed one of his more famous miracles—the multiplying of loaves and fishes, sometimes known as the "feeding of the five thousand." The Bible story says that Jesus was preaching to a large crowd who, after several hours passed, grew really hungry. All that Jesus and his disciples had with them were five fish and a few loaves of bread. Jesus told them to make a leap of faith and pass them out to the crowd, even though it seemed like it would be impossible to feed everyone with such meager offerings. Miraculously, the loaves and fishes were passed all the way around the crowd, with everybody getting something to eat, and the plates returned to the disciples with bread and fish left over.

The church built on this spot was among the places Justin had hoped to visit, to "walk where Jesus did."

Unfortunately, swarms of paparazzi photographers—some with video cameras—followed Justin and his entourage all the way to the church and then tried to push their way inside while Justin was attempting to have a moment alone in the sacred space to process the spiritual significance of where he was standing. The paparazzi's disruptive presence unsettled the pop star and his frustration grew until he spoke out—first to the paparazzi personally and then on Twitter. A video aired on Israeli TV caught a snippet of Justin's exchange with the paparazzi. He said, "Let me ask you something: Do you feel good that you're following me to a place where I'm trying to get close to God? Does that make you feel good at the end of the day? Come on."

Whenever you knock me down, I will not stay on the ground . . .

After Justin tweeted about how upset the experience had made him and threatened to hole up in his hotel room for the remainder of his weeklong visit to the Holy Land, thousands of Beliebers sprang to his defense, tweeting encouraging words to the singer and, in at least a few dozen cases, hurling nasty condemnations at the paparazzi who had so unsettled their beloved star. Hundreds more of his fans said that they were praying for him, that his trip to Israel would turn around and become all that he had hoped it would be and more. Many of their tweets contained the tag *#cheerupjustin.*

Whether it was the prayers or the kind words in his defense, Justin did cheer up, returning to Twitter (after saying he would take a hiatus from tweeting for at least a few days) to say, among other things, that "patience is a virtue." Following his well received show at Tel Aviv's Hayarkon Park on April 14,

Justin was able to continue his pilgrimage in the Holy Lands with friends and family without significant interference from the paparazzi. He visited the famed Western Wall in Old Jerusalem (sometimes called the Wailing Wall, it is perhaps the most important spiritual site in the Jewish tradition), where he left a prayer written on a small piece of paper, tucked between stones in the wall, as is the custom. He had to visit the wall in the middle of the night—3 a.m.—but at least he got his special time at that sacred place. Eventually he also was able to visit the Sea of Galilee, the Holocaust memorial Yad Vashem, and a number of other holy sites that are important to his Christian faith. All the while "the Biebs" (one of his more popular nicknames) kept his devoted fans updated on his experiences—including a kiteboarding excursion with his father, Jeremy (a.k.a. @lordbieber), and others—via Twitter.

@justinbieber, April 15-17, 2011

last night after the show i was able to see Jerusalem...really incredible experience. thank you for those who helped make it happen....

got to see the wall and the tunnels and even a sacred bath that Jesus could of bathed in. incredible. http://bit.ly/heHc1m

also got to visit Yad Vashem Holocaust Museum. An incredible place and something i will never ever forget.

now back from kiteboarding with the riders from Blade and @lordbieber @scooterbraun @adambraun and Big Erv. #BEASTS

RT @LordBieber Killing it on the sea #beast http://yfrog.com/h66qmlcuj

Israel we started off a little rough...but thank u for a week I will never forget. It's an incredible place. thank u

the fans here have been incredible...the show was amazing...and the place is truly special. My family and I will never forget this week.

• • •

On July 13, 2011, Justin surpassed eleven million followers on Twitter—more than any other user (except for Lady Gaga who has about a half-million more) on the site. That's an extraordinary number, particularly considering that he wrote his first tweet in March 2009. Eleven million is 367 times the population of his hometown of Stratford, Ontario, and about more than three-quarters the population of Ontario as a whole. His dominance of the Twitterverse (one survey says that Justin accounts for upwards of 3 percent of all Twitter traffic worldwide) is just one reflection of his meteoric rise to fame.

Plucked from obscurity in his native Canada by Scooter back in 2008, Justin's story is the closest thing to a real-life Cinderella story as you can find. In a little more than a year he went from singing to a crowd of a few dozen to selling out New York City's Madison Square Garden in twenty-two minutes. It's an extraordinary tale, one that is part of his enormous and unrivaled appeal. "He's just a normal kid" is a familiar refrain from his legion of fans. "If it could happen to him, it could happen to me" is another. Justin's fans connect with him on a level that transcends superficial infatuation. Sure, he's undeniably cute and the lad has mad musical skills, but those qualities alone don't account for his level of superstardom. Beliebers are passionate, devoted, and deeply faithful. They don't just love his music and admire the teen himself; they study both, searching for deeper connection.

When I was a teenager, if Twitter had existed and if Bono were a regular tweeter (he's not), I surely would have tracked his every move like an anthropologist studying gorillas in the mist. I would have been looking for more than just gossip and titillation. Because I admired him as much as I did (and still do), the search would have been for evidence of our common ground, spiritually speaking, and for words of wisdom and direction from a brother in the faith. Many Beliebers, at least to my eye, are doing the very same thing. In real time. All around the globe. (Tell the truth: How many times a day do *you* check Justin's Twitter feed or Facebook page? Don't be embarrassed. You're not alone.)

As someone who studies popular culture for a living, focusing particular attention on the busy intersection of culture and faith, when I spot a phenomenon as multifaceted and powerful as Justin and his Beliebers, I tend to think that there is something more going on. Something spiritual. With Mr. Bieber, that is absolutely what's happening. Rather than a pop "idol" who points only to himself, time and again Justin uses the spectacular platform that superstardom—hard-earned, humbling, and a gift from God—has given him to direct his fans toward something much, much bigger. "I feel I have an obligation to plant little seeds with my fans," Justin told *Rolling Stone* magazine in February 2011. "I'm not going to tell them, 'You need Jesus,' but I will say at the end of my show, 'God loves you.'"

At seventeen, Justin is still a kid. It's a fact he's well aware of and mentions often. While he has been raised with an abiding Christian faith—something he embraced personally, according to his mother, when he was just five or six years old—he has a lifetime ahead of him to make mistakes, stumble, correct himself, triumph, fail, and everything that's in between whether he remains in the spotlight or not. He is far from perfect, but so far at least, when he missteps, he apologizes publicly and tries to correct his behavior accordingly. In the Bible, one of the Hebrew words used most often for "sin" actually means to "miss the mark." When Justin misses his mark, he picks himself back up, recalibrates, and tries again. It's a quality that is as admirable as it is rare in anyone, especially a child on the cusp of manhood who lives in the glare of the most unforgiving, unrelenting kind of public scrutiny.

Justin has a message beyond what many critics quickly dismiss as "puppy love." But it *is* about love—*God's* love for everyone. And his fans are listening.

Rather than writing off Justin as just another flash in the pan—the latest in a long parade of young pop stars who appear suddenly and spectacularly, only to burn out and fade to black— my intention in the pages of this book is to take Justin as seriously as many of his millions of fans do. I hope to peel back the veneer of celebrity to examine the soul behind the superstar and, moreover, to take a close look at how the perhaps unlikely faith of this teenage übercelebrity is not only a key to his staggering popularity, but an influence that is shaping the lives and hearts of young people (and more than a few of their parents) around the world.

I Belieb it.

Do you?

Chapter 2

In the Beginning

Be not afraid of greatness: some are born great, some achieve greatness and some have greatness thrust upon them.

— WILLIAM SHAKESPEARE, TWELFTH NIGHT, ACT II, SCENE V

Before I shaped you in the womb, I knew all about you. Before you saw the light of day, I had holy plans for you: A prophet to the nations—that's what I had in mind for you.

— JEREMIAH 1:5

Take the story of Cinderella.

Cross it with Harry Potter.

Sprinkle in a bit of the Karate Kid.

And you might get close to the incredible story of Justin Bieber.

At only seventeen, Justin's journey (so far) is so utterly fantastic it seems like a fairy tale—so much so, in fact, that I'm tempted to begin with the words, "Once upon a time in a land far, far away . . ."

As any true Belieber worth her (or his) weight in Sour Patch Kids knows, Justin Drew Bieber was born in London, Ontario, Canada, on March 1, 1994, at 12:56 a.m. on a Tuesday.

Justin's mother, Pattie Mallette, was just eighteen years old when her son was born two weeks past his due date. Justin's father, Jeremy Bieber, was a few months shy of his twentieth birthday. Justin's parents weren't much older than he is now when he was born, a fact that he says "freaks [him] out" and that he tries not to dwell upon.

Pattie and Jeremy were engaged to be married when Justin was born, but split when he was just ten months old. Although he has always maintained a relationship with his father, Justin lived with and has been raised primarily by Pattie in the town of Stratford, Ontario. Jeremy Bieber moved away from Stratford to find construction work in a different province, and for a time lived in Winnepeg, Manitoba, nearly nine hundred miles away. When Justin's dad was able to visit him, "it was great," Pattie said. "He's a good dad. He'll discipline him when he needs to discipline him and love him when he needs to love him," she said." Jeremy has since married and has two young children with his wife, Erin Wagner: a daughter, Jazmyn (born in 2008), and a son, Jaxon (born in 2009). Jeremy Bieber and his family recently moved back to Stratford.

Being the child of parents who weren't together wasn't easy for Justin. "My dad was away at work a lot of the time, and, yeah, that sucked for me sometimes," he wrote in his 2010 autobiography *First Step 2 Forever: My Story*. "It sucked for him too. But in life you realize that the world's not perfect and if it had been up to us we'd have been together all the time. And it sucked for my mom, because being a single parent is never easy, especially with a little prankster like me. There were times when my mind went to, 'What if such and such?' or 'It could have been like da-da-da.' But, as of right now, my life is working out pretty sweet and every morning I wake up grateful for the blessings I have.

"At the end of the day, families are what they are. If you feel like a freak because you don't have a normal family, I've got news for you: pretty much nobody does. In fact, I don't know if there's any such thing as a 'normal' family."

Throughout much of Justin's childhood, Pattie worked multiple jobs—designing websites, teaching computer classes, answering phones as an office receptionist—to make ends meet for her family of two. Happily, she had a great support system in her parents, Bruce and Diane Dale, who lived nearby in Stratford, and through her friends and pastors at the evangelical Christian church they attended. Justin was a healthy, happy child full of energy. "When he was a baby he didn't stop—ever," Pattie said. "He was go go go go go go go. He was always hyper. He's still hyper. He was a *lot* of work." To this day, his mother describes him as "strong-willed," and his grandparents, the Dales, recall their grandson as a little boy who always had to be doing something. Soccer, hockey, baseball, basketball, golf, skateboarding, goofing around with his friends, and occasionally getting into a little mischief—Justin was in constant motion, ever keeping his family on its toes.

In *First Step 2 Forever,* Justin talks about how he grew up in Stratford surrounded by a large, blended family—blood, step, and "chosen."

"Our extended family is really—well, I guess 'extended' is a good word," Justin says. "My mom's biological father died when she was a baby, so Grandpa is totally her dad, but technically he's her stepfather, who married Grandma when Mom was two, which is how my mom actually ended up with a brother and a stepbrother both named Chris, because Grandpa already had kids from a previous marriage. It would suck for her stepsiblings and their kids not to be with their dad/grandpa at Christmas, so Grandpa's ex-wife and her husband come with their kids, plus cousins on this side, and stepsibs on the other side, and after a while it's pretty complicated trying to keep track of which cousin belongs to whose aunt, or who's the stepson of the great-uncle, or the grandkid of the step-aunt—and you end up realizing it really doesn't make any difference. We're all family."

> "I don't really have a religion, but I know [about Justin's faith] because I've heard about it. I like him, so I know."
> — Greta, 13, Philadelphia, PA

Stratford, Ontario, is a town of approximately 30,000 people about eighty-five miles southwest of Toronto, the capital city of Ontario province. It's a pretty normal small city, where almost everyone knows everyone else. Kind of a Canadian version of Mayberry from *The Andy Griffith Show* or the city of Springfield on *The Simpsons* with a decidedly artsy bent. (The town motto is the Latin *industria et ars* meaning "industry and art.") For six months of every year it hosts the Stratford Shakespeare Festival, the largest festival celebrating the works of the English playwright William Shakespeare in North America. Justin's hometown is, in fact, named after Stratford-on-Avon in England, Shakespeare's birthplace. Several of Stratford's streets are named for Shakespeare's plays and characters, such as Romeo (from *Romeo and Juliet*) and Falstaff (from *Henry IV* and *The Merry Wives of Windsor*).

Justin has famously said that (before him) nothing ever came out of Stratford. That's not quite true, although Stratford still is a pretty obscure locale to the rest of the world. Its

Shakespeare festival is world renowned. (The celebrated British actor Sir Alec Guinness spoke the opening lines of the inaugural play, *Richard III*, in 1953: "Now is the winter of our discontent made glorious summer by this son of York.") The great inventor Thomas Edison worked as a telegraph operator at the Stratford station of the Grand Trunk Railway for a time, the Canadian singer-songwriter Loreena McKennitt makes her home in Stratford, and it is also the birthplace of Michael G. Turnbull, the assistant architect of the U.S. Capitol, who lived there until his family emigrated to the United States when he was eleven.

Without a doubt, though, Justin is Stratford's most famous native son. But he didn't start out that way. He was just a regular kid for the first fourteen years of his life, attending school at the Jeanne Sauvé Catholic School—a French immersion school where all of his studies were taught in French—and then at Stratford Northwestern Public School (for middle school), and finally Stratford Northwestern Secondary School for part of grade nine, the last school he attended before relocating to Atlanta, Georgia.

As a little boy, Justin went to day care at the local YMCA and also spent a lot of time at the home of his grandparents where his grandmother, Diane, gave him his own room and decorated it in blue and white, the colors of her grandson's favorite hockey team, the Toronto Maple Leafs. For all of his life, Justin has been very close to his mother's parents, particularly his grandfather, Bruce, whom Justin describes as a "hockey-loving, elk-hunting, head-butting Canadian dude, tougher than anyone I know." But Bruce is as tenderhearted as he is hardheaded, a quality that his grandson seems to have inherited. "He's not afraid to show his feelings," Justin says, "and that's why I'm not afraid to show my feelings either."

In Justin's super-successful 2011 documentary film *Never Say Never*, Bruce and Diane Dale talk about their rambunctious young grandson who "drove [them] crazy" with his seemingly endless well of energy, which Pattie helped channel into sports. Justin played several competitive sports all the way through elementary and middle school, excelling as a natural athlete and earning a reputation for being fiercely competitive. "He would not release the ball," Martin Butler, who was his soccer coach for several years and also is the father of his best friend, Ryan "Butsy" Butler, said in the film. "It was the same with hockey, he would not release the puck; in soccer, he wouldn't pass the ball. "'Pass the ball,' I'd tell him. When he did, it worked out, it was great. I had to stress to him that making the goal was as important as scoring the goal." Despite his superstardom, Justin remains closest to those friends he's known most of his life, such as Butsy and his other best friend, Chaz Somers (both appear in the documentary). "I depend on my friends like a tour rigger depends on duct tape," Justin says. "You never know exactly when or how it'll be needed, but you know it'll never fail you, no matter what the crisis."

For Pattie, friends and chosen family, many of whom she met through church and other Christian circles, played a similar role, providing unfailing aid, encouragement, and love in times of crisis as well as in moments of great joy. From the time he was born until he was about six years old (when his mother joined a different church), Justin and Pattie found a spiritual family and community of friendship at Jubilee Christian Fellowship in Stratford. There, Pattie found a support system that helped her through the often trying first years of single parenthood. "I have an amazing church family," Pattie said in a 2008 interview with *100 Huntley Street*, the longest-running talk show in Canada, produced by Crossroads Christian Communications. "They just embraced me wholeheartedly and they just mothered me and fathered me. I had so many mothers and fathers who just loved on me unconditionally and just taught me about God's love and mercy.

"There were days when I had no food in my fridge," she continued. "I had no idea how I was going to get my next meal. I would just cry out to God, 'Help me! I have no food. I have no idea how I'm going to feed Justin.' There was a little bit of pride—I didn't want to go ask for help. Not saying a word. Just telling God. People would just show up at the door with boxes of food, bags of food that day and say, 'We just felt like God really wanted to bless you with some food.' I was weeping. 'You hear me! You take care of me!' I really needed a car and somebody gave me a car anonymously. The car dealership called me to come pick it up and said it was 'from God.' They wouldn't give me a name. They just told me, 'God told them to buy the car.'"

It's impossible, really, to know why or how someone else comes to have faith in God. For some people, it's the result of a lifelong search. For others, it happens in an instant, like a bolt of lightning or a tornado touching their hearts and turning them inside out and upside down. And then there are those who come to believe after watching God's hand work in their lives and the lives of others, slowly, patiently, in startling displays of grace and gentle mercy. From his earliest moments, Justin was immersed in the community of faith, bathed in prayer, and surrounded by loving believers who cared for him and his mother. In a sense, then, it's not surprising that he became a believer himself at a very young age. According to his mother, Justin made a personal commitment to Jesus Christ when he was just five or six years old. "I told him it was his decision. He couldn't make it because of Mommy," Pattie recalled. "It has to be because of your own heart. And he kept telling me that he understood. And when he was eight or nine, he wanted to be baptized. So I let him."

Jubilee church was also one of the first places that Justin was baptized into the wonder of music. Pattie is a lifelong music lover and often sang with the church's contemporary worship band on Sundays. "As a little boy, Justin was absolutely enthralled with the drums, with musical instruments," said John Bootsma, who with his wife, Patricia, is co-pastor of Jubilee Christian Fellowship. "As soon as Pattie would take him here for service, he would make his way to the drums. If they were vacant, if they weren't being used, he wanted on them. And he had an incredible sense of rhythm and beat."

When Justin was two or three, he received a djembe—a traditional African drum covered in animal skin—as a birthday present. He would whale on that thing like there was no tomorrow. But Pattie didn't think much of her son's affinity for percussion beyond it being a fun activity for her energetic child. Both of Justin's parents come from musically gifted families. His grandmother on his father's side even composes her own music. Additionally, many of Pattie's friends were musicians and when they'd hang out together, jamming and practicing songs, she often had her young son with her. "Justin, as a two-year-old, he would wander up to the stairs and just stare at Dan, the drummer in the band at the time, and he'd just be mesmerized and grab a pair of drumsticks and start hitting the stairs," recalled Nathan McKay, a neighbor and family friend whom Justin calls "The Lion King" because of his crazy beard and impressive head of big, bushy hair. "Everybody noticed that his timing was amazing. Where does this talent come from? Does he play drums? Man, you've got to get this kid a kit."

Pattie bought Justin a little plastic drum kit, and he continued to develop his drumming skills on his own until he outgrew that set around age eight. That's when Pattie's musician friends from church stepped in and organized a benefit concert at a local Stratford hotel. Justin, with his little ears pierced and a baseball hat resting on his head at a jaunty angle, looked every bit the young hip-hop star he would soon become. He had to learn four jazz songs to play with his mother's friends that night, an impressive feat for any drummer, especially an eight-year-old who'd never had a lesson in his life. Pattie's friends raised enough money at the benefit concert to buy Justin a grown-up set of Pearl drums and six months of lessons.

> "To have such a huge icon in American pop culture that loves the Lord is just incredible. It makes me appreciate him more and the fans that he is reaching. ... I think it's a great outreach for his fans."
> — Morgan, 24, Franklin, TN

Justin kept plugging away at his mostly self-taught music. He practiced those Pearl drums religiously in the furnace room of his grandparents' house. "And he was good," his grandfather, Bruce, said. He also taught himself how to play the guitar, the piano, and the trumpet, and he had a beautiful natural singing voice—one with a soulfulness well beyond his years. Pattie loved music and their home was filled with it. From a tender age, Justin would sing along with whatever his mom had playing, whether it was Michael Jackson, Sarah McLachlan, various Christian recording artists, or the soundtrack to a *Veggie Tales* movie. (Justin has said his favorite song as a youngster was the Veggie Tales tune, "God Is Bigger than the Boogie Man.")

As a kid, Justin's father, Jeremy, had, like his son, taught himself to play the guitar. Justin's musical education continued as his

dad taught him how to play classics from Bob Dylan and Deep
Purple and introduced him to rock artists such as Aerosmith,
Metallica, Guns N' Roses, Jimi Hendrix, and Van Halen. Justin's
own musical tastes tended toward R&B and hip-hop, including Destiny's Child (he famously admits to having a crush on
Beyoncé), Boyz II Men, Alicia Keys, OutKast, Nelly, and Mary
J. Blige, to name just a few. And every Sunday at church, his
faith and his growing passion for music blended as he listened
to the praise music and felt "those harmonies hanging in the
air like humidity" soaking into his heart through his skin.

> "It's really inspirational and admirable that he can be so
> open about what he believes in."
> — Rhiannon, 14, Wheaton, IL

Still, for many years Justin kept his musical skills a secret
from most people. A typical boy who wanted to be cool around
his friends, Justin was more interested in being known as a stellar athlete. Being a pop star never crossed his mind. Justin has
always been a bit on the small side for his age, and, as is sadly
often the case for many kids, at school he sometimes became the
target for bullies who thought his size would make him an ideal
punching bag. Unfortunately for them, his tormentors were
unaware that Justin's dad is a professionally trained fighter who
taught his child how to protect himself. While Justin is hardly
one to go looking for a fight, he's no pushover either and would
handily defend himself when needed. He's scrappy, stubborn,
and not about to play the victim willingly.

As he entered middle school and his confidence continued to grow, Justin could no longer keep the musical pull on
his heart hidden from the rest of the world. It was time for the
big reveal. In January 2007, he asked Pattie for permission to

enter the Stratford Idol competition, a talent contest for kids at the local youth center. It was a four-week elimination contest, and Justin made it to the final round by impressing judges with his renditions of Matchbox 20's "3 A.M.," Alicia Keys' "Fallin'," and Aretha Franklin's "Respect." And he didn't just sound good; he was a natural performer. Ever the ham, Justin won over the audience as well, getting the crowd to clap along with his songs and giving them "shout outs." By the final week of the competition, a few dozen girls had even turned up to cheer him on from the back of the auditorium or right in front of the stage, their cameras out, recording video and snapping pictures. (They were the very first Beliebers!)

When it came time for the judges to announce the winner of Stratford Idol, Justin was nervous but confident. He sent up a few urgent prayers and waited for the announcement. When the judges didn't say his name—he placed third, although for years he thought he had come in second—Justin says his heart fell out of his chest "and rolled under the piano." Despite that disappointment, the performing bug had bitten him squarely on the butt. He was hooked.

"In the Bible it says 'everything works together for good' if you love God, but there are times when it does not feel that way at all," Justin said in his memoir, *First Step 2 Forever*. "Times when you're like, 'Yo, God! This is messed up. Could you pay some attention down here?' Maybe faith is the ability to chill and trust that somebody up there got the set list right. Maybe when you're cool with whatever comes your way, the reveal actually happens, and even the bad moments can turn around to bless you."

In the summer of 2007, Justin asked Pattie whether she would allow him to take his guitar down to the Avon Theater in the heart of Stratford's Shakespeare Festival and try his hand at "busking," which is a term for playing music or performing on the street for tips. Ever the protective mother, at first Pattie was reluctant to give her blessing, but her strong-willed son persisted and eventually she agreed to let him give it a go, just as long as his grandfather was there to keep an eye on him from his car parked across the street. He made $200 on his very first day and decided that if he kept busking, he could afford to take his mother on a holiday to Disney World. By the end of the summer, he had earned $3000 and quite a following—including the name and phone number of a cute girl who dropped it into his guitar case—by playing R&B standards, pop songs, country, and Christian tunes for the thousands of tourists who flocked to Stratford for the theater festival.

Soon after Justin began competing in the Stratford Idol contest, Pattie decided to upload some videos she shot at the shows onto the site YouTube.com so that their friends and family in other provinces who hadn't been able to watch him perform in person could see how he did. On January 15, 2007, Pattie logged on to YouTube and created an account where she could post Justin's videos. She called his YouTube channel (as such accounts are known) "kidrauhl," a nod to Justin's father who sometimes goes by the nickname "Lord Rauhl." That strange moniker comes from a series of sci-fi fantasy books by author Terry Goodkind known as the Sword of Truth series. Jeremy Bieber is a longtime fan of the stories about wizards and battles between good and evil where one of the characters is named "Darken Rahl," a.k.a.

Belieber!

"Lord Rahl." How the extra "u" got in there is a bit of a mystery, but "kidrauhl" it was.

On January 19, 2007, Pattie loaded the first videos of Justin performing Ne-Yo's "So Sick" and Lil' Bow Wow's song "Basketball." (His grandmother was the first person to leave a comment for the video, saying, "Great job kiddo. Keep it up!!!") Over the weeks and months that followed, Pattie loaded a few more videos and much to everyone's surprise, the "hits" counter on the kidrauhl channel started to climb. First there were a few dozen comments, then hundreds, and then . . . thousands. It quickly became obvious to Justin that his grandmother wasn't the only one tuning in to watch him perform.

Justin's videos had gone viral, spreading like wildfire from one user to the next as friends shared the links to his videos with other friends, not by design or as part of some scheme for publicity, but entirely organically. People liked what Justin was doing. They liked his voice, his personality, and his soulfulness. People all over Canada, and soon the world, were watching Pattie's homemade videos.

And in late 2007, one of those people watching—in the middle of the night, nine hundred miles south of Stratford in Atlanta, Georgia—was an ambitious 25-year-old music promoter named Scooter.

JUSTIN: A TIMELINE

1994: Born Tuesday, March 1, at St. Jude Hospital, London, Ontario, Canada.

1998: Mom, Pattie Mallette, buys him his first drum kit.

2000: Accepts Jesus Christ as his personal savior.

circa
2000–
2006: Attends the French-immersion grammar school, Jeanne Sauve Catholic School, in Stratford.

circa
2006: Enrolls in Stratford Northwestern Public School for grades 7 and 8.

2007: January, enters the Stratford Idol talent competition and places third.

2007: January 15, Pattie Mallette sets up Justin's "kidrauhl" YouTube account.

2007: January 19, Pattie posts video of Justin singing Ne-Yo's "So Sick" and Lil' Bow Wow's "Basketball" during the Stratford Star competition on his YouTube channel.

2007: January 20, Pattie posts video of Justin singing Sarah McLachlan's "Baby" on his YouTube channel.

2007: January 29, Pattie posts video of Justin singing Alicia Keys' "Fallin' " and Aretha Franklin's "Respect" and playing drums on his YouTube channel.

2007: January 30, Pattie posts video of Justin playing a song on the electric keyboard written by his Grandma Kate.

2007: February 3, Pattie posts video of Justin singing "Refine Me" by Christian artist Jennifer Knapp on his couch at home.

2007: April 25, Pattie posts video of Justin (with a close-shaved head with swirl patterns cut into it) singing Ne-Yo's "Because of You" at home.

2007: April 27, Pattie posts a video of Justin singing Brian Mc-Knight's "Back at One" in his bathroom (before brushing his teeth).

2007: Summer, Justin starts busking in front of the Avon Theater in Stratford (and makes about $3,000).

2007: Summer, music manager Scott "Scooter" Braun discovers Justin's videos while surfing YouTube late one night in Atlanta. The next morning he tracks down Pattie Mallette and convinces her to bring Justin to the U.S. to talk about becoming his manager.

2007: June 7, Pattie posts a video of Justin singing Edwin McCain's "I'll Be" and playing guitar on his couch at home.

2007: July 19, Pattie posts a video of Justin playing the djembe (African drum).

2007: August 14, Pattie posts a video of Justin performing Life-house's "You and Me" at an outdoor concert.

2007: September 3, Pattie posts videos of Justin singing Ne-Yo's "Do You" and Elliott Yamin's "Wait for You."

2007: October 13, Pattie posts videos of Justin performing (on drums) at the Amazing Kids jam concert.

2007: November 12, Pattie posts video of Justin singing Stevie Wonder's "Someday at Christmas" in a recording studio.

2007: December 11, Pattie posts video of Justin singing the original song "Set a Place at the Table" (written by Jake Leiske and produced by Jay Riehl) in a recording studio.

2007: December 24, Pattie posts video of Justin performing "Someday at Christmas" on stage (his earliest "professional" video).

2008: February 10, Pattie posts a video of Justin singing Chris Brown's "With Brown" at home. (This is the famous video of Justin sitting on a couch with a poster of Bart Simpson on the wall behind him.)

2008: February 19, Pattie posts video of Justin playing guitar and singing Justin Timberlake's "Cry Me a River" at home.

2008: April 13, Justin signs with Island Def Jam Records.

2008: Summer, Justin spends the summer busking in front of the Avon theater and then enrolls in Stratford Northwestern Secondary School for grade 9, the last Stratford school Justin attended before relocating to the United States.

2008: Autumn, Justin and Pattie move to Atlanta, and Justin begins homeschooling through the School of Young Performers with his private tutor, Jenny.

2009: July 7, Justin releases his first single, "One Time," quickly charting in the top 20 in five countries.

2009: October 6, Justin releases "One Less Lonely Girl" exclusively on iTunes.

JUSTIN: A TIMELINE

2009: October 26, Justin releases "Love Me" via iTunes.

2009: November 3, Justin releases "Favorite Girl" via iTunes, appears for the first time on *The Ellen Degeneres Show* and launches the four-date "Urban Behavior" promotional tour with a concert in Edmonton, Alberta, Canada.

2009: November 13, Justin becomes the first solo artist ever to send four songs from a debut album up the Billboard Hot 100 charts prior to his album's release.

2009: November 15, Justin appears for the first time on *Good Morning America*.

2009: November 17, Justin releases his first album, the EP (extended play) titled *My World* (selling 137,000 copies in its first week and debuting at No. 1 on the Canadian Albums Chart), and appears on *The Ellen Degeneres Show* (for the second time in a month) and also on *The George Lopez Show*.

2009: November 18, Justin appears on the TV show *Chelsea Lately*.

2009: November 20, his appearance at the Roosevelt Field Mall in Long Island, New York, is cancelled after thousands of fans mob the shopping center and police are summoned to handle the crowds due to safety concerns.

2009: November 23, Justin opens for Taylor Swift at London's Wembley Arena in London and breaks his foot onstage (but he finished the song!).

2009: December 20, Justin performs "Some Day at Christmas" for President Barack Obama during the television broadcast of *Christmas in Washington*.

2009: December 31, Justin performs on *Dick Clark's New Year's Rockin' Eve with Ryan Seacrest.*

2010: January 18, Justin releases the new single "Baby" via iTunes.

2010: January 31, Justin is a presenter at the 52nd Grammy Awards.

2010: February 1, Justin sings the opening lines of "We Are the World" for the 25th-anniversary version of the benefit song, this time to aid victims of the devastating earthquake in Haiti. The song is released worldwide on February 12.

2010: March 10, police in Liverpool, England, threaten to arrest Justin for "inciting a riot" if he leaves his hotel room.

2010: March 23, Justin releases his first full-length studio album, *My World 2.0*, and it debuts at No. 1 on the Billboard Album chart.

2010: March 27, tickets go on sale for Justin's August concert at New York City's Madison Square Garden and sell out in 22 minutes.

2010: March 31, *Billboard* announces that 16-year-old Justin is the youngest solo male artist to top the *Billboard* chart since 13-year-old Stevie Wonder in 1963.

2010: April 10, Justin appears as the musical guest on *Saturday Night Live*.

2010: April 20, Justin releases the single "Somebody to Love" via iTunes. The song was originally recorded by Justin's mentor, Usher, who re-recorded "Somebody to Love" adding his vocals to the official remix of the song, released on June 25, 2010.

JUSTIN: A TIMELINE

2010: April 26, police in Australia cancel Justin's promotional performance at a television studio after several fans are injured in the unruly crowd gathered to see him.

2010: June 23, Justin launches his first official headlining tour in Hartford, Connecticut.

2010: July, Justin becomes the "most searched for" celebrity on the Internet and enters a recording studio in New York City to begin work on his next album.

2010: August 31, Justin plays a sold-out show at Madison Square Garden.

2010: September 12, Justin performs at the MTV Music Awards.

2010: September 23, Justin guest stars on the television series *CSI: Crime Scene Investigation* playing a "troubled teen."

2010: November 21, Justin wins four American Music Awards, including Artist of the Year.

2010: November 26, Justin releases the album *My Worlds Acoustic*, which includes the new song "Pray."

2010: December 1, Justin is nominated for two Grammy awards, for Best New Artist and Best Pop Vocal Album. (When the awards are announced in February 2011, he wins neither.)

2011: February 11, Justin's feature-length documentary film, *Justin Bieber: Never Say Never*, is released in the United States and Canada, earning $12.4 million at the box office on its opening day. According to BoxOfficeMojo.com, it is the highest-grossing concert film of all time and third-highest grossing documentary feature-length film.

2011: February 17, Justin reprises his guest role on *CSI: Crime Scene Investigation*. This time his "troubled teen" character is shot and killed.

2011: February 20-21, Justin cuts his famous "swoosh" hairstyle into a short, spikier do. The hair collected from his cut later raises more than $40,000 for charity through an online auction.

2011: May 13, DVD of *Never Say Never* is released.

2011: May 22, Justin wins six Billboard Music Awards, including Top New Artist and Top Pop Album for *My World 2.0*.

2011: June, Justin is ranked No. 2 on the *Forbes*' list of Best-Paid Celebrities under 30. He is the youngest star and one of seven musicians on the list with $53 million earned in a 12-month period.

Chapter 3

The Fairy Godmanager

God can do anything, you know—far more than you could ever imagine or guess or request in your wildest dreams!

— EPHESIANS 3:21

Somehow I can't believe that there are any heights that can't be scaled by a man who knows the secrets of making dreams come true.

— WALT DISNEY

Instead of sleeping in a cupboard under the stairs at 4 Privet Drive, Little Whinging, Justin had a blue pullout couch in a basement apartment in Stratford, Ontario. And in lieu of a fairy godmother with a magic wand and an enchanted carriage, Justin's world was transformed by a guy named Scooter with a hyperactive smartphone and a purple Mercedes.

Late one night in 2007, Scott "Scooter" Braun sat in front of his home computer in Atlanta, Georgia, watching videos on YouTube.com. His friend, the Senagalese-American rap artist Akon, had emailed him a couple of links to a performer he was hoping to help promote in the music industry. While watching the videos Akon had recommended, Scooter noticed the link for a little blonde kid singing Aretha Franklin's classic R&B hit, "Respect." A thumbnail image of the video had appeared on the right-hand side of the computer screen where YouTube suggests clips it thinks viewers might be interested in based on what they're watching at the time.

Scooter clicked on the link and a few seconds later the video of Justin singing "Respect" at the Stratford Idol competition months before, one of several videos Pattie had loaded earlier that year, began to play.

Huh, Scooter thought.

Cute kid. Decent voice. But he wasn't bowled over . . . yet.

He watched a few more videos, becoming increasingly impressed with Justin's performance and obvious raw talent. Finally, Scooter clicked on the link for Justin singing Ne-Yo's "So Sick," one of the two first videos Pattie had uploaded to Twitter back in February 2007.

"When I realized it was a twelve-year-old boy, my gut went crazy," Scooter recalled in December 2010. "He had that tone in his voice, he could play multiple instruments, he could dance."

> "I think it's a great thing for this culture to have a very huge artist who loves the Lord."
> — Morgan, 24, Franklin, TN

Scooter canceled all of his appointments for the next morning and began trying to track Justin down in Canada. He called the Stratford school board and a great-aunt that Justin had never even met, and eventually made contact with another aunt, who passed his phone message along to Pattie.

As Justin's fiercest protector, Pattie was less than thrilled to receive Scooter's message. In the months since she first posted videos of him performing, Justin had amassed a YouTube following of about 40,000 people all over the world. Not long after his viral popularity began to grow, the phone calls and emails started arriving. They came from would-be music moguls who wanted to "manage" his "career," guys who claimed to be agents who wanted to make Justin a "star," and even a producer from the U.S. daytime talk show *Maury* (infamous for conducting on-air paternity tests for troubled couples who then, invariably, duke it out on stage). Pattie, probably rightly, thought they were all a bunch of con men and ne'er-do-wells. She figured this Scooter guy, whoever he was, was just the latest in a long line of crackpots from whom she was determined to shield her thirteen-year-old only child.

But Scooter was *really* persistent. (Pattie and Justin would later come to know this inherent "noodginess" as a hallmark of Scooter's character. The guy just does not give up. He's relentless, if charmingly so.)

Pattie decided to phone Scooter back from a blocked number (so he couldn't call back), essentially just to get rid of him.

"Please, listen to me for just a minute, Pattie," Scooter said. "And then, if you don't want to hear from me again, you won't have to. I just want to say I see something really special in your son. And I see a lot of myself in him, except when I was that age I had no talent. I think I can help him."

Pattie stayed on the phone with Scooter. For two hours. They ended up talking much more about each other's values, morals, and families than they did about Scooter's ideas for getting Justin a record deal in the United States. While still skeptical—Pattie is nobody's fool—she liked what she was hearing, even if Scooter's biography was not exactly what she had expected of the person God might send to guide Justin into the music industry. Scooter grew up in the affluent New York City suburb of Greenwich, Connecticut, and was reared in a devoutly religious Jewish family. His parents—Ervin, a dentist, and Susan, an orthodontist—kept a kosher home and were deeply involved with the local Jewish community, imparting to their children a finely tuned moral compass and fervent sense of responsibility for making the world a better place. Scooter (whose Hebrew name is Shmuel ben Eliezer) has always been close to his family. He has two younger biological siblings—a brother, Adam, and sister, Liza—as well as two adopted younger brothers from Mozambique, Africa—Sam and Cornelio. Scooter's grandparents were immigrants from Eastern Europe. And his paternal grandparents were Hungarian Jewish survivors of the Holocaust. In Pattie's words: "I prayed, 'God, you don't want this Jewish kid to be Justin's man, do you?' . . . I said: 'God, I gave him to you. You could send me a Christian man, a Christian label!'"

Scooter recalls that first, tense conversation with Pattie similarly. "I got her talking," he said. "I told her, 'I'm not asking you to make a decision. I am asking you to just come and meet me. I think I can show you a world that Justin could excel in, and go beyond.'

"Here she is, a single mom, living in a small town that nobody in her family had gotten out of. I think as a young girl she had dreams of getting out, so I don't think she really believed me. She didn't want him in the music business at all because she had heard all of the horror stories."

Scooter offered to fly Pattie and Justin to Atlanta on his own dime, just so they could meet in person—no strings attached. After prayerful consideration, Pattie agreed and in the fall of 2007, mother and son boarded a plane bound for Georgia. It was the first time either of them had been on a plane. (They had no idea at the time, of course, just how many hours they would be spending on airplanes in the months and years to come, jetting off to distant lands all over the world where Justin would perform for hundreds of thousands of people and even the President of the United States—twice!)

Do you remember your first time on a plane? I sure do. I was seventeen years old and boarded a Virgin Atlantic flight from Newark, New Jersey, to London where I spent a summer as a teen missionary—I was a "mime for the Lord" in London's West End, performing skits about God in white-face paint, a bow-tie, and red suspenders (which I quickly learned were called "braces" in England, whereas "suspenders" meant a lingerie garter belt). Almost twenty-five years later, I can recall just about every detail of that flight. How my palms were sweaty and my stomach lurched when we took off, but how surprisingly unafraid I was of flying once we got going despite a terrible fear of heights; how cool I thought it was when the flight attendants handed out headphones and I could choose which music to listen to on the entertainment console in the armrest; the compartmentalized breakfast, lunch, and dinner trays with tiny cups of marmalade and cheese and real silverware wrapped in plastic; giggling with my friends as we tried on the complimentary eye shades and travel socks that came with our in-flight "hospitality" bags; looking down at the Atlantic Ocean from more than 30,000 feet in the air and spotting the coast of Ireland—the country my grandmother had emigrated from sixty-five years earlier—for the first time. I vividly recall getting a lump in my throat and climbing over my seatmate (a fellow MFTL) to try, unsuccessfully, to get a decent picture of my motherland with my camera.

On that first flight back in the summer of 1987, I jetted off to completely unknown territory with a bunch of strangers for three months in a foreign country to be a street performer (yikes!) and, hopefully, convince a lot of strangers that God loved them. I viscerally remember the mix of absolute excitement and sheer terror that swirled in my heart, mind, and stomach on that seven-hour, trans-Atlantic flight. I had no clue how my life would change—if, indeed, it would—and how the experiences that awaited me in London would shape my life for many years to come. Justin and his mom must have been feeling similarly on their five-and-a-half-hour flight from Toronto to Atlanta. Excited. Worried. Nervous. Stoked. Anxious. Maybe even more than a little scared. Surely a swirl of emotions surrounded them as they deplaned and walked through the Hartsfield-Jackson International Airport terminal, not knowing exactly what awaited them on the other side of the baggage claim.

Well, a purple Mercedes-Benz CLK with a 215-horsepower engine, spinners, and chrome rims, for one thing. Scooter arrived in what Justin would dub the "Purple Pimpmobile" to collect Justin and Pattie and take them to his home in Atlanta, where they were staying during their visit.

A word about the famous purple pimpmobile, which, for diehard fans, holds an almost mythic place in Bieber legend. I was dying to know the back story myself, figuring Scooter had rented it to impress Justin—which it did. The real story is much better:

When Scooter was a freshman at Atlanta's Emory University in the late 1990s, he was short on cash and, not wanting to ask his parents for money, was looking for a way to subsidize his flagging bank account. He ended up getting involved in promoting parties at Atlanta nightclubs that catered to the college crowd. He was so good at it that the first time he threw a Thursday night party at the Paradox Theater in Atlanta's Buckhead neighborhood, more than eight hundred people showed up (and he turned a $600 profit in one night!). "I've always had a knack for building hype," Scooter said.

Pretty soon he was hooked and his bank account was more than flush. By the end of his college freshman year, he was pulling in $5,000 to $10,000 from each party he threw. Scooter continued to host hugely popular college parties at nightclubs around town, and he also started hanging out at a club called the Velvet Room, where heavy hitters from the city's bustling hip-hop and R&B music scene—such as Ludacris, Fat Joe, and Sean "P. Diddy/Puff Daddy/Diddy" Combs—hung out. Scooter didn't just want to promote parties anymore. He saw an opportunity to get involved in the business side of the music scene.

> "He's not trying to advertise Christianity or anything. He's just trying to say, 'It's okay. You have a voice. And you can have faith.' But he's not trying to say, 'Be like me 'cuz I'm Justin Bieber.'"
> — Hailley, 15, Wheaton, IL

At age twenty, wanting to impress some of the record industry guys he was trying to befriend, Scooter decided he needed a sick ride that would give him some street cred. "I thought that if I wanted to play with these [hip-hop] guys that I had to play like them. So I needed a car like they had," he said.

He found one. On eBay.

"I bought a Mercedes-Benz. It was called Aqua Blue," he said. "I will never forget it. I was bidding from my buddy's room in a frat house. Literally, bidding in the frat house. 'I think I'm going to get this car.' My friends were like, 'No way, dude.'"

Way.

Scooter won the car—for $35,000 in cash—and two weeks later it arrived at the frat house. In retrospect, it probably wasn't the wisest decision he's ever made. "I definitely got criticism for it," he said in a 2011 interview. "You've got to understand that the priorities of a twenty-year-old and the priorities of a twenty-nine-year-old are so different." When pressed about what inspired him to look for a flashy, impressive ride in the first place, the answer Scooter gave was surprising: "Because I saw the movie *Schindler's List*."

Wait. What?

Schindler's List is the 1993 Academy Award-winning film directed by Stephen Spielberg about Oskar Schindler, a German businessman who is credited with saving the lives of more than a thousand Jews during the Holocaust by employing them in his factories.

And that connects to the purple Benz how, exactly?

"At the beginning of the movie Oskar Schindler didn't have anything so he created an element of illusion that he did," Scooter explained. "He had personality, and charm; and he dined and partied with the Germans. He let the German government fund his operation [that saved so many Jewish lives by letting them] think he was somebody he wasn't."

Thus the Purple Pimpmobile was born.

Whether it accomplished what Scooter hoped it would with those hip-hop fellows or not, half a decade later his purple ride made a big impression on a young kid from Canada arriving in the United States for the first time. Justin's reaction when he saw the car at the airport was, "Sweet!" Pattie added, "Nice wheels," as Scooter loaded their luggage into the trunk.

The trio's first stop that day was at a recording studio run by producer Jermaine Dupri (who was Janet Jackson's boyfriend at the time). Scooter had known Dupri for a number of years, meeting the young music mogul on the scene while he was promoting nightclub events. Dupri eventually asked Scooter to work for him in the marketing department of his record label, So So Def. By the time Scooter turned 21, he was named So So Def's executive director of marketing while continuing to do his nightclub thing. As a club promoter (a title Scooter dislikes), his star continued to rise. He ended up throwing parties not just in Atlanta, but also in New York, Los Angeles, and Miami for clients that included the NBA All-Star Weekend, 'NSYNC, and Britney Spears.

> "I think it's awesome that as a 17-year-old, he's willing to speak his mind and say what he feels he needs to say when a lot of people won't— or they'll be very, like, political about it and try not to give it a point. But he is willing to."
> — Tamara, 20, College Station, TX

After six years of promoting parties, around the time he turned twenty-five, Scooter decided he'd had enough and walked away. He also resigned from So So Def Recordings. He had learned the ropes from some of the music industry's heaviest hitters, honed his skills in marketing and promotion, and wanted to make a name for himself on his own terms. He wanted to discover and represent new artists, fresh performers that he believed in and wanted to share with the world.

In 2007, Scooter signed Asher Roth, a white rapper from Philadelphia majoring in elementary education at West Chester University of Pennsylvania, to his new SchoolBoy Records label. Scooter found Asher on MySpace, where the young rapper uploaded homemade videos of himself performing original raps in his dorm room. Asher's debut album, *Asleep in the Bread*

Aisle, released in 2008 (not long after Scooter discovered Justin on YouTube) and sold more than 360,000 digital downloads in its first month. Scooter's new label had its first success story, and he had the serious street cred he long desired.

When Scooter, Pattie, and Justin pulled up to Dupri's studio that afternoon in late 2007, Scooter cautioned Justin that it was just a "friendly visit" and that he wouldn't be singing for anybody that day. Scooter had a plan and wanted to introduce his latest find to Dupri and others in the industry carefully, choosing just the right time, place, and presentation. "Be cool," he told Justin, just as a black SUV pulled up in front of the studio and Usher stepped out. Usher (a.k.a. Usher Raymond IV) is one of Justin's musical heroes. In fact, he auditioned for the Stratford Idol competition with Usher's song, "U Got It Bad." Before Scooter or Pattie could stop him, Justin hopped out of the Purple Pimpmobile, walked right up to Usher, and asked if he could sing one of Usher's songs for him. It was pretty cold out that day in Atlanta (although maybe not for a Canadian), and Usher basically patted Justin on the head and said something like, "Maybe some other time, little buddy." It's a story that is well known in Bieber lore, an anecdote that's been retold in scores of interviews as well as in Justin's autobiography and documentary film. It never fails to draw laughter from folks who know how the rest of the story goes, and it's a moment that Justin seems determined never to let Usher live down. (When Scooter later chastised him for approaching Usher, Justin argued that Scooter had told him not to sing for Dupri, but hadn't said anything about Usher.)

That day, the three of them ended up hanging out with Dupri, just chilling and playing video games. At some point, Justin launched into a rap and—despite Scooter throwing some serious shade—Dupri was so impressed he grabbed his video camera and asked Justin to do it again. When Justin tried to actually *sing* for Dupri, Scooter gave him the full-on stink eye and it was clearly time to leave. It was a good first visit, leaving Dupri intrigued, but Scooter warned Justin that they wouldn't be taking any short cuts. He wanted to do things right, in the proper timing. Justin and Pattie visited for a few more days and then headed back to Canada with a plan to continue uploading videos to YouTube to "organically" grow his fan base. They celebrated Christmas in Stratford with their large extended family and greeted the New Year with prayerful hope and anxious anticipation about how God's plan for Justin would continue to unfold.

For weeks, Pattie would shoot and load videos of Justin performing to YouTube, and then she and Scooter would stay up late watching numbers on the hits counter climb higher and higher. On February 10, 2008, Scooter attended the 50th Grammy Awards in Los Angeles. That night, Pattie was preparing to load the now-famous video of Justin sitting on a couch in his grandparents' house singing Chris Brown's "With You" with a poster of Bart Simpson hanging on the wall behind him. Justin killed the song, but he had just received a rather unfortunate modified bowl haircut and thought he looked like a dork. (He kind of did.) Pattie sent the video to Scooter at the Grammys for his feedback before uploading it. He sent a text in response, saying that Justin sounded amazing but the hair was so bad that they should wait until it grew out and shoot a new video. Unfortunately (or providentially, depending on how you look at it), Scooter's text got cut off and Pattie only saw the first few words, "This is really good." She loaded the video. By the time Scooter called to ask her to take it down, it already had 25,000 hits. Within a month, Justin's bad-hair day video had amassed a million hits.

Over the next months, Scooter would fly Justin and Pattie to Atlanta now and then to meet with various music industry folks. But nothing solid was coming together. They kept getting the same response: there is no way a teenage singer can break through without being part of the Disney machine or having his own show on Nickelodeon. Not gonna happen. Scooter kept trying to convince the powers that be that Justin already had a substantial fan base on YouTube—more than a million hits and counting—but no other performer had successfully launched a music career based on Internet exposure alone, so record company honchos kept showing him the door.

> "He is one of a few very professed Christians in the music industry, and I think he sets an amazing example."
> — Carl, 20, Chicago, IL

One night on the phone with Scooter, Justin vented his frustration about how slowly things were going for his fledgling career.

"Nothing great ever came that easy," Scooter told him. "This is going to happen . . . The only thing that can stop you is you. People who fail in this business—the really talented people, I mean—it's never about the music. It's about their personal lives. Stay focused and never mind any of the crap anybody says. That's not you; that's them. That's the negative place they want to live in. You choose to live in a positive place."

Like any teenager, Justin was worried about what his friends in Stratford would think if things didn't happen more quickly. They'd make fun of him, say that he was a poser, a fraud, or think he was an arrogant jerk.

"Maybe they're jealous because you have something to believe in?" Scooter said.

• • •

In the weeks that followed, there were more trips back and forth to the States for Justin and Pattie. Scooter worked every angle like the serious "hustla"—as his admirers in Atlanta's hip-hop scene called him—that he is. Eventually, things began to move. Justin Timberlake and Usher (see?) both courted Justin in the hopes of signing him to their record labels. And then it happened.

The moment of truth.

On April 13, 2008, in the New York City offices of Usher's mentor, Island Def Jam Records CEO Antonio "L.A." Reid, Justin got his first record deal.

After traveling to Atlanta again several weeks later to officially sign the contract with Island Def Jam, Pattie and Justin returned to Stratford to begin preparations for their move to Atlanta. The whole process of moving to the United States involved reams of bureaucratic red tape and took much longer than anyone had expected. So Justin spent the summer busking again in front of the Avon Theater and in the fall of 2008, began ninth-grade classes at Northwestern Secondary School with the rest of his buddies. While Pattie waited for the immigration paperwork to be finalized, she sold most of their belongings and they moved in with her parents, Bruce and Diane Dale. Meanwhile, in Atlanta, Scooter found an apartment for them a block away from Asher Roth's pad and signed the lease himself.

Finally, after what seemed like years of waiting, it was time to go.

"We said goodbye to Grandpa and Grandma and all of our friends—everything we'd ever thought of as home," Justin recalled, "and headed for Atlanta with nothing but our clothes and my guitar."

Once again, waiting for them when they arrived to spirit them into uncharted territory and a new life, was Scooter—Justin's fairy godmanager—and his dream machine.

Chapter 4

A Wing
of Protection

I regard no man as poor who has a godly mother.

— ABRAHAM LINCOLN

*God reward you well for what you've done—and with a
generous bonus besides from God, to whom you've come
seeking protection under his wings.*

— RUTH 2:11

While the first seventeen years of her son's life consti-
tute something of a fairy tale, Pattie Mallette's early
life, from her birth to the birth of her son, was quite
the opposite.

Patricia Elizabeth Mallette was born into a troubled family. Her biological father, who she says abused her mother for a
decade, left the family when Pattie was three years old. He died
a few years later. Her mother, Diane, remarried Bruce Dale, the
man whom she considers her true father. Her sister was killed
by a car when she was five years old, and from the time Pattie
herself turned five until she was about ten years old, she was a
victim of sexual abuse.

Like far too many girls and young women who are victimized by sexual abusers, Pattie kept the criminal acts against her a secret for many years. "It was just sort of known that you don't say anything," Pattie told the Canadian Christian television program *100 Huntley* in June 2008. "You didn't want to ruffle the feathers and cause trouble and hurt people, so you sort of take it and hide." Pattie has not revealed publicly the identity of her abuser.

"As a little girl, I sort of just kept bottling it up and kept it inside," she said. "But when I became a teenager that's when I sort of started exploring with drugs and alcohol and some things to try to relieve the pain that way, and just experimented with crime and the wrong kind of people—just trying to do anything to get some joy or something, some sort of pleasure. I was pretty much high or drunk from the time I woke up to the time I went to bed. I started when I was about fourteen or fifteen."

Searching for a sense of belonging that she didn't find in what she described as a "pretty broken home" where the hurt prevented her from forming strong bonds with her family, the friends she found in the drug culture became her community, the place where she was known and fit in, however wrong-headed that was in hindsight.

"You try stuff and you want to sort of fit in and you want to be around everybody," she said. "But it becomes about what it's filling inside you or what you think it's filling inside of you and it's sort of just masking the pain . . . When you're addicted, it takes over your life. You're selfish. You don't care about any[thing] else but your own satisfaction."

At age fifteen, Pattie left home.

"I didn't really get along with my parents at all. I ended up living in a home with several guys. There were four guys, I think.

I just lived a life of sin. Drugs and alcohol constantly and parties constantly. And not going to school. And stealing. Just my own world," she recalled. "The relationships I was in [then] were definitely not healthy relationships by any means. Not physically abusive, but definitely emotionally very unhealthy."

Things came crashing down around Pattie when she was seventeen. She had reached the end of her rope: mired in despair and weighed down by depression, she decided she no longer wanted to live.

"I had just had enough of everything. The abuse from my childhood was built up for so long, and just keeping that a secret for so long, and all the drugs and all the alcohol and all the life I was living and just the bad relationships I was in. I was depressed and angry and I just snapped one day. I said, 'I want to die.'"

Pattie wanted to find the "quickest way possible" to kill herself, but she didn't have a gun or access to pills that might hasten her death. However, she did live on a busy road and settled on killing herself by stepping in front of a passing vehicle.

"I ran outside—I thought I timed it perfectly," she said. Down the road she saw a truck hurtling toward her. She ran in front of it, but the driver saw her and swerved at the last second. "There was a side street. He slammed on the breaks and turned down the side street. I was so angry and embarrassed and ashamed that I didn't get hit. It was crazy. I was a teenager just hurting, just wanting to escape."

Rather than an escape, Pattie found herself locked up in the psychiatric ward of a local hospital. It was during the first days of her stay there that reality of how false the "community" of the drug culture she had clung to smacked her in the face. "I didn't have any friends come visit me," she recalled. "I really didn't have any friends at that point."

But Pattie was not alone. The Hound of Heaven was pursuing her, and he was hot on her heels. In 1909, the poet Francis Thompson published a poem titled "Hound of Heaven." In it he described how God pursues his lost sheep. Relentlessly, like a hound chasing a hare, God chases after his children, never giving up hope that they will turn around and embrace him. Thompson described the way so many of us run away from God like this:

I fled Him, down the nights and down the days;
I fled Him, down the arches of the years;
I fled Him, down the labyrinthine ways
Of my own mind; and in the mist of tears
I hid from Him, and under running laughter.

Blessedly, God never, ever gives up pursuing us. The faster we run, the faster God runs. The farther we go, the farther God goes. When we try to hide, God finds us. When we ignore God, God waits for us to change our minds. And God has way more patience and stamina than we do.

Eventually, Pattie did receive a visitor, a man named John who she knew in passing from a youth center where she used to occasionally hang out. John worked for the Christian organization Youth for Christ.

"We used to have talks about God here and there," Pattie said. "He ended up coming in to visit me in the hospital and he brought me a rose, he brought me a flower. I thought, *Okay, people bring people flowers in the hospital. That's nice.* Then he told me, 'I want you to know that God told me to bring this to you, and he wants you to know that he sees you like this rose.'"

Sometimes the Hound of Heaven carries a rose in its teeth.

"I was thinking, *Oh my gosh, this man obviously doesn't hear from God—if God's even real—because I am not a rose. I am living in sin. I'm stealing. I'm sleeping around. I'm doing drugs and alcohol. I am not a rose to God,*" she said.

Undeterred by Pattie's resistance, John kept on talking about God and how much God loved her and how she was precious to God, beautiful, wonderfully made, perfect, like a rose. And he kept coming back to visit, bringing fast food from McDonald's and Kentucky Fried Chicken, hoping outside food (way tastier than what was served in the hospital) would make her more open to listening. He was right. She listened, nodding graciously between handfuls of French fries, but really just humoring him.

"He would talk to me about God, and I would really, in my heart, be rolling my eyes, thinking, *Man, he talks a lot about God, and it's not even Sunday!* . . . He said a lot of things that made sense, but I thought, *That's really great for you, and it's great that it works for you, but it's not for me.* One day he just said, 'You tried to kill yourself. You don't even want to live any more. You don't want your life. God created you with a plan and a purpose. What do you have to lose by giving God a chance to see what his plan is for you, what he can do for you?' I couldn't even roll my eyes in my heart at that one. I was just stumped. I was at rock bottom. I had nothing to lose by giving him a chance, if he's real. I really didn't think God was real."

> "Justin Bieber has more sway over people right now than any pastor does, which is sad, but he actually has so much more impact on these young people. I'd be interested in seeing if Justin actually realizes that—and that he can make a bigger impact on our generation than a lot of people can."   — Tamara, 20, College Station, TX

After John left that day, Pattie went back to her hospital room. She stared up at the ceiling and thought about praying, but wasn't quite sure how to start. So she just started talking.

"I kind of looked up and said, 'Okay, God, if you're real, I pray that you would come into my life and . . . what John said— come in and live my life for me. Live my life through me because I can't do it and I don't want to do it. I'm tired. I'm exhausted. Show me. And Jesus, if you're real and you can come and you can forgive me all my sin . . .' And then, all of a sudden, you know how people say when you die your whole life flashes before your eyes? For me, it was like every sin I'd ever committed flashed before my eyes. And I was like, 'Oh God, if you can forgive me, if I'm not too far gone, if it's not too late—and if it is I understand because I've been, ya know, pretty bad.'"

> "I'd be curious to know how Justin's superstardom affects his faith."
> — Annie, 20, Wheaton, IL

While she was praying, Pattie had a vision of her heart. It opened up and in poured tons of glitter (she calls it "sparkle dust"), so much that not even a single speck more could fit. The glitter was love, "God's love," she said.

"And then it closed and it turned bright, bright, bright white, like I had been completely purified and completely cleansed," Pattie said. In the television interview, as she tells the story, Pattie puts her fingers together in the shape of a heart. It's the same "heart" hand gesture that millions of Bieber fans around the world make to show their allegiance to and love for Justin. I'd always wondered what the origin of the famous Belieber heart gesture was. Pattie's divine vision of God healing her heart appears to be the answer.

Even though she was alone in her hospital room, Pattie said she felt a powerful presence. She wasn't alone. God was right there with her. "I was like, 'Oh my God, you're real! Oh my God, you're real!'" Pattie said. "I just kept repeating this by myself. 'Oh my God, *you're real*!!' I was weeping and crying. 'He's forgiven me and I'm clean and he's *real* and he loves me!'"

Pattie ran to the hospital phone and called John. "I said, 'God . . . is real.' And he said, 'Yeah? What happened?' I said, "No. No no no. I don't think you understand. I don't think you know. I know you've talked about God, but *God is real*!' He said, '*I know! What happened?!*'"

Pattie explained what she'd just experienced at the hospital and John rushed over to see her again, bringing her a Bible of her own in a modern English translation (the King James Bible she had pulled from the drawer of a desk in her hospital room was written in an old-fashioned kind of English—lots of "thees" and "thous"—that was difficult for her to understand), and he prayed with Pattie. "I remember saying in the prayer, 'God, if I follow you and I have you in my life, I know you don't like drugs and alcohol, and I really like my drugs and alcohol. So you better be better than drugs and alcohol because I don't want to give it up if you're not better.' I was talking to God like that. So raw and so real."

For the next week or so, Pattie walked around "high on God." No drugs or alcohol, but the highest high she'd ever experienced in her life. She started reading her Bible regularly and attending church, walking with God in this brand-spanking new life God had given her.

Now, for those of you who have also experienced God's spectacular presence and power in the sort of way that Pattie did that day in the hospital eighteen years ago, let what happens next be not a cautionary tale for you (although it certainly could be), but a reminder of how great and bottomless God's grace and mercy are. Even Jesus' own disciples, who lived with him in the flesh, believed what he said, and heeded his call to spread the gospel, still were human and made mistakes. Epic mistakes. St. Peter himself, one of Jesus' closest friends, stumbled in his faith and denied even knowing his Lord—not once, but three times—on the day he was crucified. Opening the door of our hearts to let Jesus in means we're forgiven, but it doesn't mean we're perfect. When we doubt, fear, or are simply rebellious, we can still get into a heap of trouble. But Jesus promises to be by our side in those moments, walking with us, carrying us when we need to be carried, and ever ready to offer us grace again and set us back on the right path.

So even when we meet God the way Pattie did, we still have the choice to walk away. (Can you hear the barking and paw beats right behind you? Yeah, I thought so.)

"About six to eight months after my initial experience with God . . . I hooked up with some old friends, people that I hung out with, partied with and stuff. I ended up starting to get back into drugs and alcohol again and the old life. I started going to church a little less and a little less . . . and I ended up pregnant," Pattie recalled. "I thought, *Oh my gosh, I took my life back into my own hands, and I'm all by myself and I'm pregnant. God, help me. I give my life back to you wholeheartedly. I don't ever want to go back to that life. Please, will you please, please take me back and help me raise my son?*"

Pattie said she was ashamed of going back to church as an "unwed mother," but she knew that's what she had to do, as horrifying as it might be to face people who might judge her harshly. "I had no other choice," she said. "I knew what the alternative was and it's not good. So I was like, 'God, you have to help me.' And he did."

Thankfully, the church Pattie chose to return to was Stratford's Jubilee Christian Fellowship, where the congregation was committed to meeting people exactly where they were, no matter the circumstances, with heaping servings of love rather than judgment.

> "First of all, [Justin's faith] will spread Christianity, hopefully, to some of his fans. It will make people want to be a Christian more. Since he shows it so well, it will help us know what to do when we're Christians."
> — Sarah, 14, Franklin, TN

Of course, the baby that Pattie was pregnant with was born on March 1, 1994. Pattie and Jeremy Jack Bieber, the baby boy's father, gave him the name "Justin," which means, in Old English, "just, upright, and righteous." When Pattie and Jeremy split while Justin was still an infant, the folks at Jubilee came up around Pattie to support and love her in whatever way she needed. They mentored her, brought her food, gave her good counsel, and even bought her the car she so desperately needed to get to the two jobs she worked in order to support her baby boy.

Pattie and Justin attended Jubilee church until Justin was about six years old, when Pattie chose to join a different faith community. But even years later, having relocated to the United States in 2008, she and Justin stay in touch with their spiritual family at Jubilee.

"We have a relationship with Pattie," John Bootsma, co-pastor of Jubilee Christian Fellowship, said in a 2011 interview with the *100 Huntley* television program. Pattie is an "intercessory prayer warrior," meaning she believes passionately in the power of prayer and prays in organized groups with other men

A Wing of Protection

and women who pray specifically for the needs or concerns of others. For years she's maintained a private prayer list that she shares with close confidantes, including members of Jubilee. "We lift them up at least weekly and sometimes more often," Bootsma said. "We feel like God has his hands on Justin and Pattie for such a time as this. And we recognize the influence he's got. So we pray for him. Prayer is powerful."

The episode of *100 Huntley* in which Pattie shared the awesome story of her spiritual journey was taped in June 2008, not long before she and Justin moved to Atlanta, Georgia, to work full-time on Justin's musical career. At the time, Justin was fourteen years old. "He's not just healthy, but he is talented and he's so beautiful and he's so gifted and he just has the biggest heart and I'm just so unbelievably blessed and I don't deserve it one bit from my own doing or anything I've done," Pattie gushed, bragging on God, really, rather than on her remarkable child.

"It doesn't hurt to give God a chance, even if you don't know if he's real. God says, 'Search for me with your whole heart and you will find me.' He doesn't say you 'might' or 'if I feel like it.' He says, 'if you seek me, you will find me,'" Pattie says. "If you will just give God a chance with your heart, he will show up. I promise. He will."

Chapter 5

Praying
It Forward

Pray, and let God worry.

— MARTIN LUTHER

| @studiomama | Jul 2 2010, 6:15 | @armyofprayerwar thanks! pray protection over us and God's plans and purposes to prevail |

J ustin's mother Pattie is an intercessory prayer "warrior," meaning she is deeply committed to praying for
other people, places, situations, and even entire nations.
Like many Christians—evangelical Protestant and Pentecostal
Christians in particular—Pattie believes that through prayer,
believers can engage in spiritual combat, literally coming against
the powers of evil in the name of Jesus.

For those who don't come from the kind of religious tradition that Pattie and Justin do, spiritual warfare sounds almost
like science fiction—strange, weird, and difficult to understand.
In the Bible, St. Paul is credited with writing a large portion
of the New Testament, including a number of "epistles," or

"letters," to new churches and communities of believers in the first years after Jesus' death. One of those letters, to the church in Ephesus, is known as the book of Ephesians. In it, St. Paul explained what it means to do spiritual battle, through prayer, this way:

God is strong, and he wants you strong. So take everything the Master has set out for you, well-made weapons of the best materials. And put them to use so you will be able to stand up to everything the Devil throws your way. This is no afternoon athletic contest that we'll walk away from and forget about in a couple of hours. This is for keeps, a life-or-death fight to the finish against the Devil and all his angels.

Be prepared. You're up against far more than you can handle on your own. Take all the help you can get, every weapon God has issued, so that when it's all over but the shouting you'll still be on your feet. Truth, righteousness, peace, faith, and salvation are more than words. Learn how to apply them. You'll need them throughout your life. God's Word is an indispensable weapon. In the same way, prayer is essential in this ongoing warfare. Pray hard and long. Pray for your brothers and sisters. Keep your eyes open. Keep each other's spirits up so that no one falls behind or drops out.

The kind of battle-prayers St. Paul is talking about in those verses from Ephesians is often called "intercessory prayer." The word *intercessory* means to act as an intermediary between two people. In the Christian tradition, intercessory prayer means praying to God on someone else's behalf. In other words, in prayer, you are acting as a go-between for God and another person.

> "I don't think it's wrong for people to pray. I just … have a hard time wrapping my mind around the fact that prayer could actually do something, besides just having kind thoughts toward somebody."
> —Anna, 13, Philadelphia, PA

In certain Christian traditions, intercessory prayer means specifically praying to God on behalf of people in the world who are not physically present. In other words, they're praying for the world beyond their doorstep, for people and places that they cannot see but can still reach—and help protect—in the spiritual realm.

Pattie believes in the power of prayer to change the course of history, to physically heal people who are sick, to comfort those who are suffering, and to help turn the hearts of people who are running away from God back toward God and God's love. God doesn't "make" us do anything. Since God created us with "free will," we are capable of making our own decisions—good, bad, and ugly—including whether to believe in God. When God created human beings, God wanted something different than the angels, who are God's servants. God wanted children—companions, really—who could *choose* to love him back rather than be programmed to do so, like robots. We're a lot like God, in that way. Wouldn't you rather be loved by someone who wants to love you, rather than someone who loves you because they feel obligated to or because they "have to"?

How prayer actually works is a divine mystery. It's not a magic wand or a secret handshake. Nor is it like putting together a desk from Ikea, where, at least in theory, if you follow the directions precisely, the outcome is always the same.

According to Søren Kierkegaard, the Danish philosopher who wrote extensively about the Christian faith, "Prayer does not change God, but it changes the one who offers it." Prayer can bring about a change of heart, it would seem, for those who are running from God as well as for those who are praying for them.

How prayer "works" in the spiritual and physical realm is mysterious, but I know for sure—and Pattie does too—that it is powerful. It can "move mountains," the Bible says. "Absolutely everything, ranging from small to large, as you make it a part of your believing prayer, gets included as you lay hold of God," Jesus said.

♥ ♥ ♥

In "Never Say Never: For Nothing Is Impossible with God," a twelve-page discussion guide for churches and communities of faith, published to accompany Justin's 2011 documentary film, *Never Say Never*, Pattie spoke boldly about her faith in the power of prayer.

"As a woman of faith and a praying mom, I would pray often about God's plan for Justin's life and mine, having no idea at the time just how BIG His plans were," she wrote in the guide's introduction. "Truly nothing is impossible with God. He called us to be a light in this world and has provided more than what we needed."

"The power of prayer is effective," she wrote, citing James 5:16. "And we depend on it. Prayer has been an important part of Justin's life since childhood. . . . The film's title is fitting because Justin never gives up on his dreams. He keeps on dreaming despite the many obstacles and challenges he's faced in his young life. With all that's happened in these last couple of whirlwind years, the phrase will always have a special meaning for us. Never say never, for nothing is impossible with God."

@studiomama	May 15 2011, 17:20	He replied, "What is impossible for people is possible with God" Luke 18:27.

Just before *Never Say Never* was released in theaters on February 11, 2011, Pattie sat down with the folks from the Hollywood Prayer Network for a series of interviews about her son, their shared faith, and what she believes is God's special call on Justin's life.

Founded in July 2001 by television producer Karen Covell, the Hollywood Prayer Network (www.hollywoodprayernetwork. org) is a grassroots network of more than 10,000 intercessory prayer warriors around the world who are committed to praying for people working in the Hollywood entertainment industry. The goal of the network is to provide spiritual support to both Christian believers and nonbelievers who work as actors, producers, directors, writers, technicians, support staff, crew, and in other positions in television, film, music, and other mainstream media.

Since early 2011, the Hollywood Prayer Network, at Pattie's request, has been asking intercessors to pray for Justin. They've even set up a Facebook page where people can post their prayers for Justin, his family, and his professional team. The network even has a button on the front page of its website that allows readers to tweet their prayers and support for Justin on Twitter.

"Justin is 17 years old and has become a global phenomenon, not yet understanding that celebrity can be more of a curse than a blessing," the website explains. "His mom asked that we pray for both of them, to keep their eyes on Jesus, to make wise decisions and not be swept into the dangerous mindset that fame and celebrity suck people into. . . . Let's be a part of praying Justin into a continued safe place with the Lord, no matter how much the industry pulls on him! Would you join us in covering this young man, who is currently the most popular star in the world, and his mom, who is trying to handle his life, career, schooling and spiritual training?"

The network's list of specific prayer requests for Justin include:

- For his voice, as it is hard on his vocal cords to be singing as much as he is.
- For his safety and well-being as his fame increases. Let's surround him with prayer so that he stays grounded in his Christian faith, never loses sight of the fact that his gifts are God-given, and resists the growing pressures he's facing to embrace a secular lifestyle.
- That the Lord would continue to give him creativity and grace to be faithful with what God has asked him to do.
- For guidance and wisdom as he does media interviews. Justin needs wisdom and great preparation to know how to answer the difficult questions that the interviewers will purposely throw at him. It's very hard for a [seventeen]-year-old to know how to handle the press and so we need to ask the Lord to speak through him and to give him preparation needed to be wise and confident when in public. And may the Lord bring him the right coaches to guide him in this process.

In addition to the prayer warriors at the Hollywood Prayer Network, Pattie has folks back home in Canada—at Jubilee Christian Fellowship in Stratford and elsewhere—who regularly support Justin in prayer. She is also careful about the people who surround Justin professionally and are the closest to him, as she explained in her interview with the prayer network.

"We are very selective about the core team and who's around him," Pattie said. "His manager [Scooter Braun] is really protective of that as well. His manager . . . is of Jewish background and has great values and good morals and tries to instill them in Justin. We have a lot of [good people] around us . . . I also have some Christian people around him. We had a travel pastor come on tour with us a lot. So he has people like that in his life. Justin's got a Christian tutor now. I always have my friends coming around, and men of God speaking into his life.

"I have several pastors that I go to and I bounce some things off of people that I trust [for] their wisdom and their support," she continued. "It's really important that we keep Christian people around him, godly influences and good influences that will help keep him grounded and protected and not doing anything stupid . . . Kenny [Hamilton], his security guard, would never let him go to a club, would never let him go and do drugs or drink or anything like that. So, there are people around him who I trust, and I think that's really important."

> "I would pray that he never changes and that he glorifies God through everything he does, which he is right now. And that he'll continue to grow in his faith … and in his fame as well."
> — Susanna, 14, Nashville, TN

Of course, we know that Pattie has been praying for Justin since before he was born. And well before he took the first steps toward superstardom, his mother covered all of her decisions for her young son in prayer. Even with her prayer and those of her church and support system, making the choice to allow Justin to pursue a career in the music industry was not an easy one. But now, she says, she has a peace about the unexpected path her son's life has taken.

"I do have peace now because I prayed so much into it, and I had so many people praying with me," she said. "At first I was like, 'God, surely this isn't your plan for him' . . . You see all these stories about people getting into all kinds of trouble, and it's just not the best environment to raise a child in. . . . So praying about it . . . I kept having this peace, even though it's a real struggle for me because I thought it just went against my paradigm and how I figured God was going to use him.

"And God said, 'I called you to be a light in the world. How are you supposed to be a light in the world if you're not in the world?' And then it was like, oh, okay. But even then I was struggling [with], well, should we be doing it in the Christian music industry? Is that the direction that you want us to go? But just praying through it, it was clearly, 'No.' It's supposed to be an evangelistic tool, and the Christian music industry is geared just to Christians mainly, so we really felt like this is the direction [we're supposed] to go," she said.

Still, Pattie's doubts and fears lingered. "'But God, I have roots,'" she recalled praying. "'He's still young. He's just still growing and still trying to figure out who he is and who you are.' And God's like, 'Trust me. Trust me.' [God] just kept bringing me back to the [Bible] story of Samuel and Hannah and Eli. Eli didn't exactly get [the] Father of the Year award, but he was supposed to trust [God] with Samuel. And God just kept saying, 'Trust me. Trust me. Trust me.'"

| @studiomama | Jul 15
2010, 7:37 | RT @andrewakemp: @studiomama when did you accept Jesus Christ as your personal savior? - When I was 17 years old! Best thing I ever did. |

According to Pattie, Justin made a personal commitment to Jesus Christ at the tender age of five or six. A few years later, he asked his mother if he could be baptized and, after she quizzed him on the meaning of baptism for a Christian believer and felt sure he understood its importance, Justin was baptized.

Like so many believers who meet and embrace Jesus at a young age—or any age, for that matter—Justin's faith walk has its ups and downs. I made a commitment to Jesus for the first time when I was about ten years old. My mother and father had become born-again Christians after joining a Bible study when I was in grade school. My mother, a fortress of spiritual strength, was eager for my younger brother and me to embrace their new faith as well. But I was, as I mentioned earlier, a strong-willed child. I was precocious, bright, and inquisitive, and I had my own questions about God, faith, and Jesus. If I was going to find the answers, it was going to be in my own sweet time. My whole family began attending a Southern Baptist church when I was in fifth grade. There I heard the pastor preach about God's love for us and God's grace that was a free gift. All I had to do was accept it. All of my sins—past, present, and future—would be forgiven and my heart would be brand new (just like Pattie saw in her vision in the hospital).

So after a few months, I began to understand what Jesus was all about, but I hadn't made a final decision to open the door of my heart. I'm not sure exactly what I was waiting for, but when the moment came, it arrived in the most surprising way. Late one Sunday night, I couldn't sleep, which was unusual for me—as a child, I was a champion sleeper. In retrospect, something must have been troubling my heart. I got out of bed and went downstairs to the den, where my mother was watching a church service on TV. I sat next to her on the couch and began to watch the sweaty preacher teach the same kind of message I'd heard a number of times before at church. After a few minutes, my mother got up to go fix herself a cup of tea. The TV preacher continued to deliver his passionate sermon, shouting and crying and sweating profusely. (What is it with TV preachers and flop sweat?) Still, I listened to what he was saying and it struck a chord in my spirit in a way it hadn't before. When he invited his congregation out in televisionland to pray a prayer with him, giving their hearts and lives to Jesus, surprising no one more than myself, I prayed it too.

And that's how I got "saved," in the middle of the night, alone in front of the idiot box, watching the Rev. Jimmy Swaggart preach his sweaty gospel message. I was ten years old, so the experience didn't lead to immediate or dramatic changes in the way I lived my life. Nevertheless, that moment was life changing for me. I can look back thirty years later and see how the orientation of my heart shifted, how I had access to a kind of peace that I can't explain other than to say it's a gift from God that sustains me even in the very worst of times. (And I've had a few.) When you make the most significant spiritual commitment of your life as a child, the rest of your spiritual story tends to be a lot less Disney and a great deal more real. Each of us has to find our own path through life and walk our own journey with God. Sometimes the way is straight and smooth. Other times it's a series of hairpin turns down the side of a mountain (without any brakes). That's what it means to be human. Jesus understood this too. He walked in our shoes. He knows what it's like to feel pain and sorrow, joy and excitement, fear and doubt. And he promises to be with us every step of the way.

> "I think Justin and his family stay closer through praying. I liked that they all are friends on tour. He seems down-to-earth, but when you know his story, he has God-given talent :) and he makes me smile when he smiles! We sang his songs at my birthday sleepover and I love all his songs!! He connects to people all over the world." — Carly, 16, Vernon Hills, IL

Justin is blessed to have a mother who understands this too, and who doesn't freak out when his walk is shaky or when it looks like he might be heading off the beaten path. I have to believe that it is her faith—imperfect, messy, real, and beautiful—that allows her son to embark on his own spiritual journey with such palpable grace, knowing that wherever he goes, Jesus is by his side. So at age twelve, when Justin told Pattie that he didn't want to go to church services on Sunday any more, she didn't argue with him, realizing, perhaps, that church is not the only place where he would encounter the holy.

"He's trying to find himself, and he's trying to find God," Pattie told a newspaper reporter in February 2011. "He's sixteen. But God has hooks in his heart. He's still on his own journey. Mine is mine, and he can't have mine. He needs his own." That said, when the reporter asked Pattie what she thought God's purpose was for Justin's life, Pattie didn't miss a beat in answering. "His purpose is to be the voice of an entire generation. To raise up the standard. . . . To raise the standard in a moral way, whatever that means."

Pattie is keenly aware that some Christians want Justin to use his fame explicitly to bring souls to Jesus Christ and that some of them don't think her son is going about it the right way. "I know a lot of Christians want to evangelize and bring people to God, but I believe that parts of Justin's spiritual journey may not look the way religious organizations want them to look," she said.

"I'm aware of the dangers," Pattie said, of her son's career in pop music. "He's my son, and I'm accountable to God and by the law to protect him—which includes covering him spiritually. Justin's faith is strong, but he's young and hasn't come completely into himself yet. So what I can do is pray, teach, and continue surrounding him with strong Christian influences."

One thing Pattie is sure about is that Justin realizes his musical abilities and career are both a gift from God and a ministry that he must work hard and be careful to honor. "He definitely knows that he is not here on his own merit and on the hard work of people around him, although we have hard-working people around us and he has worked very hard and done his part. He cannot deny the unprecedented favor of God in such a short period of time," she told the Hollywood Prayer Network in early 2011.

Pattie sees God's fingerprints all over Justin's life—and heart.

"It's been such a whirlwind. He does not deny the fact that God is the one that is orchestrating all of this and giving him such incredible favor," she said. "And he knows that it's for a purpose and a plan. He's not sure what all that entails yet and how he fits into that, but he knows that it's by God's hand."

Belieber!

THE FAITHFUL MOTHER

Pattie Mallette, Justin's mother, joined Twitter in February 2009, a month before her son did. With more than a half-million followers, Pattie is an avid tweeter herself.

Over the years, Pattie has used her Twitter account to quote scripture and inspirational quotes from Christian men and women, such as C. S. Lewis (the author of the Chronicles of Narnia, among many others), to offer spiritual encouragement and guidance, and to ask for, offer, and call for prayer.

Here is a selection of Pattie's tweets, chronicling the heart of a woman of God and a faithful, faith-filled mother.

@studiomama	Feb 4 2009, 16:39	Reading the Bible and doing laundry. Whooo hoo.
@studiomama	Jul 15 2009, 6:54	Reading the book of JOB in Seattle. Can't sleep. Sleepless in Seattle :P
@studiomama	Nov 24 2009, 1:06	Yes Justin fractured his foot but he's so amazing he finished the song limping onstage! Thx 4 all the prayers!!! He's in a cast for 6 wks.
@studiomama	Apr 22 2010, 4:34	Japan is beautiful but jet-lag is not so fun!! Jesus revive and re-energize us!!!!
@studiomama	May 9 2010, 9:32	Wisdom is worth much more than precious jewels or anything else you desire." http://read.ly/Prov8.11.CEV

@studiomama	Jun 25 2010, 1:54	Justin's show is so amazing! So proud!!!! God has been so good to us! Jeremiah 29:11
@studiomama	Jul 2 2010, 5:48	@wbgenie you never know unless you try! God gives you gifts & desires for a reason. Its not always how we think He will use it tho. Bless u!
@studiomama	Jul 2 2010, 6:41	@Pattiesarmy traveling is great!! miss my bed sometimes, but I'm making memories! God is good!!
@studiomama	Jul 2 2010, 6:43	@JDianaBieber thanks! He needs it :) We all need it. Pray for the bus driver too, driving thru the night! We need angels watching over us 2!
@studiomama	Jul 3 2010, 3:57	RT @Patties_Army: @Studiomama your correct on that. We all need an army of prayer warriors.
@studiomama	Jul 5 2010, 8:40	@kelsidarlingxo - The LORD is close to the brokenhearted; he rescues those whose spirits are crushed Psalm 34:18
@studiomama	Jul 10 2010, 5:42	RT @JUST1BIEB: @studiomama Wow #fathersloveletter explains Him and what He does so well..AMEN
@studiomama	Jul 13 2010, 20:24	RT @JbieberPrayers: God I pray that today be productive and blessed! I cover your people and @justinbieber
@studiomama	Jul 14 2010, 9:17	Honestly had the time of my life 2day/2nite w y'all from @thecitychurch & http://thecity.org - @judahsmith & friends blessed me SO much! TY!
@studiomama	Jul 15 2010, 0:13	RT @Djsikes96: @studiomama what iz ur fav Bible verse? - Jeremiah 29:11 - what is your's?

@studiomama	Jul 15 2010, 7:52	RT @iYiYi_LoveCodyS: @studiomama is my savior! -- NO thx! I will be a role model but never anyone's savior. That's what God is for!! :)
@studiomama	Aug 7 2010, 5:39	I need prayer everyday for increased wisdom, understanding, knowledge & revelation.. esp. wisdom 4 direction & words! In Jesus name! Thx!!!
@studiomama	Aug 7 2010, 14:31	Thx!! - RT @TESSALILIAN: @studiomama I think there are alot of people praying for u. God has touched people's hearts so ur always supported
@studiomama	Aug 8 2010, 6:01	Thx!! Pray for a husband for me please!! Haha. Why did she have to pick Roberto!? RT @_huliaa: @studiomama praying for you!
@studiomama	Aug 8 2010, 6:09	HAHA!! YES! She's so blessed! God has mine out there somewhere! Plz pray! RT @lAURENicoleX3: Praying for @studiomama!! ROBERTO? seriously??
@studiomama	Aug 8 2010, 6:12	So right!! Never need one ladies! God is all I need. I sure would like one tho!!
@studiomama	Aug 10 2010, 13:56	RT @CSLewisDaily: God, who foresaw your tribulation, has specially armed you to go through it, not without pain but without stain -CSLewis
@studiomama	Aug 14 2010, 23:06	@emskyxx Happy bday! God knew u before He planned creation! 2morrow is a GOOD day & He has good plans for u!!
@studiomama	Aug 15 2010, 4:55	RT @CSLewisDaily: It is safe to tell the pure in heart that they shall see God, for only the pure in heart want to - C.S.Lewis

@studiomama	Aug 16 2010, 0:41	Pray & pretend God loves you & that He has an answer for you until you know it, because He does. - Bob Hartley
@studiomama	Aug 17 2010, 3:26	Gone for a few days away by myself 2 seek God & His heart, & shutting off my phone. Please pray for me
@studiomama	Aug 21 2010, 5:42	If God is for you, who can be against you? Romans 8:31
@studiomama	Sep 3 2010, 7:16	As the heavens are above the earth, so my ways are higher than your ways & my thoughts higher than your thoughts. - Isaiah 55:9
@studiomama	Sep 3 2010, 7:45	@marcelolobo thank you!! God is a Redeemer!! Glad u were moved
@studiomama	Sep 8 2010, 6:48	Forgive your parents. They are not perfect but they sure do love you. Honor them & God promises to give you a long full life! Deut. 5:16
@studiomama	Sep 8 2010, 6:57	RT @USBieber: @studiomama i was actually mad at my dad, but i thinkim gonna go tell him i love him right now, thanks(: -- that's so great!
@studiomama	Sep 8 2010, 7:00	@OzBelieber I know what its like 2 have ur dad leave, but God is the perfect Dad who will NEVER leave u. He's able 2 fix that ache! Just ask
@studiomama	Sep 8 2010, 7:01	RT @Tarabieber__: @studiomama Yesterday I was mad at my mom, but I said I love her. ;D - good stuff!
@studiomama	Sep 8 2010, 7:04	@AldinaLuvJustin your Daddy in heaven loves you very much. He sent Jesus to die so you could know His love for you if you will accept it!

@studiomama	Sep 16 2010, 8:30	RT @KennyHamilton: I'm about to lay it down! Good night all! Say your prayers... - gnite!!!
@studiomama	Oct 5 2010, 0:31	RT @JustinDimples: I wannna thanks @studiomama for makin believe in GOD more than I used to.I pray every-night
@studiomama	Oct 5 2010, 15:32	Good morning Daddy. What shall we do today?
@studiomama	Oct 5 2010, 15:37	That's my hearts desire!! RT @thist-wit13: i wonder if @studiomama knows how many people she's made believe in God.
@studiomama	Oct 5 2010, 15:57	Yay! RT @kirstendonn: i just read the bible because of @studiomama (:
@studiomama	Oct 9 2010, 19:22	Doing what u believe is right, is very hard sometimes. God will honor your sacrifice. God please help me.
@studiomama	Oct 24 2010, 1:44	God works ALL things together for good for those who love the Lord & are called according to His purpose! Romans 8:28
@studiomama	Oct 24 2010, 3:12	That defeats the whole purpose of scripture if I do that! Gotta spread the word not keep it contained!!
@studiomama	Oct 25 2010, 3:54	God won't allow us to go thru more than we can handle! Even if it feels like its too much, He knows we are stron-ger than we think we are!
@studiomama	Oct 25 2010, 4:00	I think God is squeezing me to make oil. It hurts but it will be worth it. What's that saying? What doesn't kill u makes u stronger!

@studiomama	Oct 25 2010, 6:14	I like that! Good night twitter world! RT @poidog123: @studiomama God would never put us through something he couldnt get us through :)
@studiomama	Nov 12 2010, 7:34	I am royalty. I have destiny. I have been set free. I'm gonna shake history. - Jake Hamilton.
@studiomama	Nov 23 2010, 6:45	Psalms 30:12...I'm about to burst with song; I can't keep quiet about you. GOD, my God, I can't thank you enough!
@studiomama	Nov 23 2010, 6:49	RT @CSLewisDaily: God's love is not wearied by our sins & is relentless in its determination that we be cured at whatever cost to us or Him
@studiomama	Dec 13 2010, 14:46	So full."My cup runs over" I'm rich w true genuine friends. That's what really makes u rich is love in any form. So grateful. U know who u R
@studiomama	Dec 13 2010, 20:38	Its not too hard for God. Keep praying!!
@studiomama	Dec 20 2010, 4:33	Do u believe in miracles? Can God thru prayer heal people?
@studiomama	Dec 25 2010, 16:37	Merry Christmas & Happy Holidays!! Happy Birthday Jesus!!!
@studiomama	Jan 4 2011, 7:13	Give away your life; you'll find life given back, but not merely given back— given back with bonus and blessin. . . http://bible.us/Luke6.38.MSG "Don't pick on people, jump on their failures, criticize their faults—unless, of course, you want the same treatment

@studiomama	Jan 14 2011, 16:17	Let no corrupting talk come out of your mouths, but only such as is good for building up, as fits the occasion. . . Do you have the nerve to say, 'Let me wash your face for you,' when your own face is distorted by contempt? I. . . http://bible.us/Luke6.42.MSG
@studiomama	Jan 14 2011, 22:07	RT @bobhartley: The Lord wants to bring beautiful companionship and friendship in areas where people don't feel cared for.
@studiomama	Feb 2 2011, 7:16	Psalm 4:7&8 You have given me greater joy than those who have abundant harvests of grain and new wine.
@studiomama	Feb 6 2011, 14:01	"Don't pervert justice. Don't show favoritism to either the poor or the great. Judge on the basis of what is. . . http://bible.us/Lev19.15.MSG
@studiomama	Feb 28 2011, 7:08	With him is an arm of flesh, but with us is the Lord our God, to help us and to fight our battles.
@studiomama	Apr 21 2011, 8:45	Love is patient and kind. 1 Corinthians 13:4 Lord help me love!!!!
@studiomama	Apr 23 2011, 5:05	The moment u embrace lack in someone elses life is the moment u embrace lack in your own life.
@studiomama	May 15 2011, 17:19	@negativecolors Thanks for hanging on. Its hard but worth it! So glad I could bring u hope! With God all things are possible! I believe in u
@studiomama	May 16 2011, 2:29	@negativecolors Don't ever apologize for your appearance. You're beautiful. God says you are "wonderfully & perfectly made" (psalm 139:14)

@studiomama	May 16 2011, 7:22	If you want to go higher, you must go lower. Those who humble themselves will be exalted.
@studiomama	May 26 2011, 5:14	Good night world. TRUTH = God LOVES you. Praying for dreams from God tonight!!! Agree w me? Thanks for all ur prayers!! We really need them!
@studiomama	May 27 2011, 5:41	Why do we kick ppl when they're down? Don't Judge. Pray 4 them instead! Its hard but "Do not Judge or you too will be judged." Matthew 7:1
@studiomama	Jun 6 2011, 14:37	Know therefore that the Lord your God is God, the faithful God who keeps covenant and steadfast love with those who love him and keep his commandments, to a thousand generations,
@studiomama	Jun 17 2011, 6:49	A fool is quick-tempered, but a wise person stays calm when insulted.
@studiomama	Jun 21 2011, 4:01	Come on young ppl! Let's raise up a standard 4 a generation. Kids honoring parents - friends honoring each other. #whatdoeshonorlooklike ?
@studiomama	Jun 21 2011, 4:11	Let's create a culture of honor ppl. Men be an EXAMPLE 4 ur sons 2 honor mom by truly demonstrating honor 2 ur wife. #whatdoeshonorlooklike
@studiomama	Jun 21 2011, 4:40	@Dee_Lulu14 No such thing as "just a teen". Teens have a voice & a msg. U can be a revolutionary generation. Lead w Love, Integrity & HONOR!

Chapter 6

His World

It's a big, big world
It's easy to get lost in it

— JUSTIN BIEBER, "UP"

Don't panic. I'm with you. There's no need to fear for I'm
your God. I'll give you strength. I'll help you. I'll hold
you steady, keep a firm grip on you.

— ISAIAH 41:10

When Pattie and Justin moved to Atlanta in late 2008, they knew almost no one there besides their new BFF, Scooter. One of the first people they met was Kenny Hamilton, an Atlanta DJ and longtime acquaintance of Scooter's who would join Justin's team as his bodyguard and a central figure in the chosen family mother and son created in their newly adopted hometown.

Kenny is a gentle giant of a man with a broad smile and easy demeanor. But woe to anyone who mistakes Kenny's inherent kindness and tender spirit for weakness. The man could stop a freight train with his bare hands if it meant keeping Justin out of harm's way. Also, when the situation warrants it, he can pick Justin up like a rag doll and run with him. (And he has, often for fun and occasionally out of necessity.)

Pattie actually spoke with Kenny long before she and Justin relocated from Canada to the United States. One day on the phone with Scooter before visiting Atlanta for the first time, Pattie asked about nearby churches they might be able to visit while they were there. Scooter is Jewish, so this wasn't exactly his area of expertise. But Kenny happened to be in the room when Pattie called, so Scooter said, "Here, talk to Kenny—he goes to church" and handed his large friend the phone.

"Sure, I'll take you to my church," Kenny said.

When Justin and Pattie arrived in Atlanta with little more than their clothes and his guitar, they moved into an apartment Scooter had rented for them not far from where his other client, rapper Asher Roth, lived. Even though Asher is a number of years older than Justin, Scooter figured at least he was a friendly face in the neighborhood who could show them around—here's the best supermarket, that café makes the best lattes, etc.—and keep a brotherly eye on fourteen-year-old Justin. "I'm gonna watch you, bro," Asher warned Justin. "I don't want you splashing money around and getting into nice things. You gotta stay humble about it." No worries, Justin told him, and jokingly added, "I'll just have people walking behind me throwing flower petals everywhere I go."

While Pattie and Justin arrived in Atlanta during the school year, they decided that Justin would work with a tutor from the School of Young Performers, which specializes in homeschooling children working in the entertainment industry, rather than enrolling in a local high school. Because he wasn't in a "regular" school and with the demands of his increasingly busy schedule—vocal training, choosing the material he would eventually record, and strategizing about how best to introduce his music to a global audience—Justin found it challenging to make friends in his new city. Kenny stepped in, spending loads of time with his new charge and getting to know him better by bowling, shooting hoops, and just hanging out. They quickly formed a tight bond that continues to this day—playmate, protector, and adopted uncle in equal parts.

Kenny guards Justin's physical safety, makes sure he's on time for his myriad appointments and obligations (a Herculean task given the young pop star's penchant for goofing around), and generally keeps him out of trouble. "I also try to make sure that I watch out for his character," he says. That last part is the number one priority for everyone on the Bieber team, especially Pattie.

"I don't care about the money; I don't care about the fame. I care about him being a good person," she said. "I don't want to just surround him with 'yes men.' I want him to still have that sense of perspective and to be grounded and to know who he is. If you're not a good person, what's it worth, ya know?"

When it came time to choose a vocal coach for Justin, the choice was obvious: Jan Smith, a.k.a. "Mama Jan," a legendary vocal trainer in Atlanta who had been brought in years before to help Usher regain his voice after it broke during puberty, and he thought he might never sing again. Plainspoken and smart as a whip, she has a well-earned reputation in the music industry as an Olympic-level vocal coach, working with such musical luminaries as Rob Thomas of Matchbox 20, Keyshia Cole, Collective Soul, Jill Scott, and, of course, Usher. Mama Jan is about the farthest thing away from a "yes man" you could find. Scooter calls her "the special sauce," and she may ooze Southern charm, but she does not suffer fools gladly. She is the Mr. Miyagi to Justin's Karate Kid. Justin might be able to bat his impressive eyelashes, stick out his bottom lip, open his huge puppy-dog eyes (à la Puss in Boots in the *Shrek* movies), and get away with murder with most people, but not Mama Jan. And like Kenny, she also is a person of faith who shares the values that Pattie was most concerned about fostering as her only child entered this exhilarating and daunting new chapter of his young life.

"He's kind of a really big influence on everybody because to all of his fans that watch him and follow him on Twitter or Facebook or anything, he's a big person that they look up to. And when he puts that he can believe in God and still be able to have this amazing life, it shows people that anybody can have that."   — Bridget, 16, Crystal Lake, IL

While Justin got to work with Mama Jan, training two or three times a week, Scooter and Pattie were busy growing his fan base online, loading new videos on his "kidrauhl" YouTube channel, and watching the numbers climb. Justin was eager to get right into the recording studio, but Scooter was determined to take his time, cautiously searching out the right songs for Justin's debut on the world stage.

Many months before, when Justin approached his hero Usher in the parking lot outside Jermaine Dupri's Atlanta studio, the reigning King of R&B remembers telling the kid he mistakenly believed to be Scooter's younger cousin, "If it's truly meant, then we'll meet again." And meet again they most certainly did after Scooter worked his extensive connections in the city's music scene to arrange a meeting between Justin and Usher in the studio.

"When I heard his voice for the first time, I thought, *This is going to be a musical journey that people are going to remember for a long time,"* Usher said. He quickly became one of Justin's most ardent supporters. He saw a lot of himself in the Canadian teen and wanted to mentor him through the next phase of his life and career. "If you're an astronaut going to the moon, there's not a whole lot of people with whom you can share that experience," Usher told Justin. "I can talk you up and get you back down safely. The beautiful part of all of this is you don't get a chance to see it while you're in it. Now I actually get a chance to step back and watch it all happen again. Those incredible moments on stage . . . even the obstacles, it'll be a pleasure to watch, even though it's agonizing, you know. But I can be more helpful because I've experienced that. Being the entertainer I am, I stand on the shoulders of giants that basically were trailblazers. And all of my experiences, I want to share."

Usher was the same age as Justin when L.A. Reid signed him to his first record deal. When Usher was coming up, Reid sent his personal assistant at the time to work closely with Usher, teach him the ropes, and guide him through his earliest days in the business. That person happened to be Sean "Diddy" Combs. Usher thought Justin could use the same kind of a life coach/ style guru that he had as a youngster, so he sent his own personal assistant, Ryan Good, to work with Justin.

Ryan is perhaps best known as Justin's "swagger coach," the genius behind Justin's signature color purple and unique sartorial style—a mix of hip-hop/rock star/boy-next-door—with his color-coordinated skater sneakers, baseball lids, and jeans that somehow manage to be both skinny and saggy-in-the-butt at the same time. Officially, Ryan is Justin's tour manager, but unofficially he is also his court jester. Fans will probably recognize him as the guy who makes Justin laugh harder than anyone else, popping through doorways shouting his goofy "COME

AWN!" They may also know him as the dude with purple-and-pink ponytails sticking out from the top of his head in the viral video of Justin pranking his tour mate, Willow Smith, on stage while she sings her hit, "Whip My Hair."

With the addition of Ryan, Team Bieber was complete and Operation Justin was in full swing with the lad working long hours in the studio laying down tracks for the first time and Scooter leading a charm offensive with L.A. Reid to convince the record company president that it was time to start releasing music to the public.

The first song Justin recorded was "Common Denominator."
When broken hearts line up to say love is a lie
You and I will stand as love's reply, yeah

It was the first of many love songs Justin would record in the coming months, all of them a delicate balance between universal feelings about relationships—love, loss, infatuation, excitement, insecurity, pain, joy, fear—and song scenarios that were age-appropriate both for the boy singing them and his fans, most of them girls in their teens and tweens. Once Reid heard the song, he gave the thumbs up for Justin to record a full album. By the time the Grammy Awards rolled around in February 2009, Scooter flew to Los Angeles armed with a CD of ten songs to play for Reid at his bungalow at the Beverly Hills Wilshire Hotel. As the story goes, Reid is a very busy man and rarely listens to more than a couple of songs, three if you're really lucky. But when Scooter started to play Justin's songs for him, Reid listened to all ten—and then asked Scooter to play them again. Justin's first album, *My World*, got the green light.

Justin had a great time shooting his first video for the single "One Time"—he even flew best friend Ryan "Butsy" Butler down from Canada to be in it with him (he's the kid sitting next to Justin on the couch in the opening scene)—and the plan was to release the video via iTunes on a Tuesday morning not long before the single itself went on sale. Something went wrong at iTunes headquarters and the song was released, without any marketing or publicity, late on a Friday, two weeks early. Scooter was not pleased, thinking it a business disaster. Justin had just set up a Twitter account a few weeks earlier, so he logged on and sent his first tweet:

@justinbieber	May 12 2009, 3:27	Check out my single "ONE TIME" on my myspace and spread the word for me. Thanks www.myspace.com/justin-bieber

By the following Monday, "One Time" was the No. 3 video on iTunes. By Tuesday it was No. 2, behind Taylor Swift. On July 7, 2009, the "One Time" single dropped to a huge response, quickly charting in the top twenty in five countries. In October, he released "One Less Lonely Girl" and "Love Me," and on November 3, "Favorite Girl." Ten days later, Justin became the first solo artist ever to send four songs from a debut album up the Billboard Hot 100 charts before the album was even released.

By the time Justin's first album, the EP *My World*, dropped on November 17, 2009, his already massive fan base was champing at the bit. *My World* sold 137,000 copies in its first week and by the end of that year, more than 850,000 copies of his debut albums had been sold worldwide. During the ramp up to and release of his album, Justin began making his first appearances on national television in the United States—*Ellen, Good Morning America, Chelsea Lately,* and *George Lopez.* For the first time in his life, fans started recognizing Justin everywhere he went.

On November 20, Justin was scheduled to appear at the Roosevelt Field Mall in Long Island, New York. When thousands of fans mobbed the place, overwhelming mall security, the police stepped in and asked Justin to cancel the event before he could even arrive at the shopping center. The fans were crazy, pushing and shoving and knocking down security barriers. Five people were taken to the hospital for minor injuries. It was a terrible scene. Police arrested an executive from Justin's record label and charged him with endangering the lives of minors. Eventually police also charged Scooter with two misdemeanors—reckless endangerment and criminal nuisance—because police said he didn't follow their orders to send out a tweet to fans calling off the event fast enough. (The charges were dropped in May 2011 after Justin agreed to record a public service announcement about the dangers of cyber bullying.) The media started referring to Justin's growing celebrity as "Biebermania," comparing it to the frenzy that greeted the Beatles when they made their debut in the 1960s. Somewhere during that time, the press gave Justin's millions of passionate fans a nickname: Beliebers.

Justin's world had changed more dramatically and faster than anyone could have imagined. But his virtual overnight success wasn't the only thing changing in Justin's life. He was getting older too, and like any teenager, there were growing pains (and not just for him).

"At fifteen, sixteen, nobody can tell you anything," Usher said. "You're 'the man.' Having this type of recognition and success is a lot to balance." Pattie seconded that emotion saying, "He's a typical teenager, so he pushes his boundaries."

Case in point: When it came time for Justin to get his driver's permit, he headed to the local department of motor vehicles to take the written test without once having cracked the "Rules of the Road" handbook. Scooter and Pattie tried to suggest that he might want at least to take a look before the exam, but Justin thought he already knew all there was to know about driving. Well, he failed the test—by one question—and when he came back to the car where Pattie was waiting to drive him home, he refused to get in. If he couldn't have a permit because of some stupid test, then he wasn't about to ride in a car. It was raining. He didn't care and started to walk home. Pattie kept pace in the car, shouting through the open window for her son to get in. This went on for some time—Justin walking along sullenly in the rain, yelling at other drivers for driving poorly ("And THEY get a license!"), and generally feeling embarrassed and wronged for going home empty-handed, before he finally agreed to get back in the car.

Justin is a nice kid. But sometimes—like every other teenage boy on the planet—he doesn't like to listen to his mother, he sulks when he doesn't get his own way, and his mood swings are at the mercy of his raging hormones as much as his vocal cords are.

> "I do think it's good that big pop stars like Justin Bieber talk about being a Christian and stuff because it's a good influence on me. Especially because he's in the spotlight a lot, it's kind of hard for him to come out with being a Christian and stuff. But then he's also a good role model because of the way he acts." — Camille, 14, Nashville, TN

There's a telling moment in the 2010 *E! News Special*, "Justin Bieber: My World," where Pattie glares at him from across a crowded room with her enormous blue eyes and shouts, "You're not allowed to eat Big Macs!" while Justin ignores her and proceeds to scarf down the sandwich, the hood of his sweatshirt pulled so low on his head that it hides his eyes.

"I can't exactly ground him," Pattie says. "We haven't been

home in more than a year." Instead, Pattie confiscates his cell phone and laptop. Once she even cancelled his mobile phone plan when he wouldn't give up the phone. Of course, cutting Justin Bieber off from technology has its own special consequences that go beyond having a surly teen on their hands.

"If he isn't on Twitter for a day, his fans are like, 'Oh my God! Did something happen to him? Why isn't he tweeting?'" Kenny said, chuckling. "Well, he was probably on punishment and his mom took his phone." Unlike most teenagers, however, when Justin disappears from the Twitterverse for a day or two, rumors of his death start to spread and occasionally wind up being reported by CNN.

"In some ways I think it's a typical mother-and-child relationship," Mama Jan said of Pattie and Justin. "I think the difficulty now is that Justin is a superstar; it is very difficult for a mom to fight the world. So it's a tough, tough, tough job for her."

Team Bieber tries to make Justin's life as normal as possible given the extraordinary circumstances. "He wants to date and does, and his team tries to protect him that way [and tries] very much to provide those normal opportunities to him," Mama Jan said. But it's a challenge to offer Justin "normal" when some of his fans behave so bizarrely. "Some of the mothers offer themselves to security or other people on the team in an effort to get their daughters closer to Justin, and I'm like, 'Well, that's a great example you're setting,'" she said.

"It worries me that there are actually older women—and I don't know whether they're joking or what—[who are] flirting with Justin and will express inappropriate things to him," Pattie said. "Obviously as a mom, nobody wants that for their son . . . He's expressed his desire to stay pure and honor women and treat women with respect, so hopefully that stays that way."

Pattie is not as concerned about his younger fans—even the girls who scream and cry and push to try to get close to him and say they want to marry him some day. "Most of the young ones—most of the young girls—it's innocent," she said. "They just have a crush."

However, every once in a while even the younger fans behave in a way that troubles Justin. "One time, I was really disappointed," Justin said. "I saw this girl—she was a big fan and was [standing] outside. So I got out of the car and gave her a big hug and she tried to kiss me. I was like, 'Why are you trying to kiss me? I just came and gave you a hug. Shouldn't you try and respect me?' "

As the summer of 2010 approached, Justin braced himself for new levels of fame and encounters with thousands more fans all over the world. On June 23, 2010, in Hartford, Connecticut, he launched his first world tour in support of his first two albums, *My World* and *My World 2.0*, which were released four months apart, the second in early 2010. He played more than one hundred concerts in twenty countries between June 2010 and May 2011 and also shot a feature-length documentary film about the tour—his 2011 biopic *Never Say Never*—at the same time. It was a grueling schedule and sometimes being on the road and away from family and friends took its toll on him.

"Everyone is waiting for you to screw up, and everyone wants you to be what they want you to be, twenty-four hours a day," Scooter said. "Sometimes he wants to be that kid back in his room, but he understands the blessings. However, it is tough, especially for a teenager—and the hormones are raging. He's definitely become more guarded than he was four years ago."

Ryan "Butsy" Butler and Chaz Somers, Justin's best friends from Stratford, fly to meet the singer while he's on tour as often as they can. But they're "regular" kids who attend a normal high school, so their visits are not as frequent as any of them would like. Still, when his boys are in town, Justin isn't interested in introducing them to lifestyles of the rich and famous. He just wants to play ball, whether it's hitting the basketball courts at Chelsea Piers in Manhattan or playing a pick-up game of soccer in Spain. Butsy, Chaz, and other friends from his "old" life help keep his feet planted on the ground, and more than that, they are confidantes—people who know and like him because he's Justin the person, not the superstar. As his celebrity continues to grow exponentially, finding ways to do "normal" things with his buddies or his girlfriend, Selena Gomez, is increasingly challenging. He can't catch a movie with Selena without it becoming an international media story. Even a trip to the Scoopers ice cream parlor in Stratford takes almost Secret-Service-level planning to get him in and out without being mobbed by fans or paparazzi.

"It's his biggest struggle at times, and he handles it very well," Scooter said. "But I think it's scary to him . . . to think that, maybe, for the rest of his life that he is never going to be normal again."

> "I was wondering if Justin is as big on faith as he seems, or is it all made up to make him look better?"
> — Peyton, 13, Muncie, IN

Thankfully, Justin has a close friend who can understand how steep the learning curve is between Stratford and super-stardom. Usher has been there. He knows what it's like to be where Justin is today and how to navigate through the difficult times. "There's a great reward in it, but there's also a great sacrifice," he said. "That sacrifice is that you might not necessarily have the time to hang out with your friends . . . I told him, 'I'm here. I'm not only someone who you're in business with. I'm someone who loves you. I want to make sure that this business does not consume you.' The business has robbed many, many, many, many artists of that childhood experience. I don't want him to lose that."

From the outside, at least, it looks like Team Bieber is doing a stellar job of helping Justin enjoy the time he has left as a teenager. For every Justin sighting at an awards show or television program, there are almost as many reports of the pop star at play, watching a basketball game with friends or a professional fight with his dad, going fishing with Kenny or camping with his family, a trip to the mall with Selena or catching a concert at a small club in suburban Southern California. Even when he's spotted with other celebrities, it's not usually for a power lunch at a Los Angeles restaurant where they're sure to be photographed by the paparazzi. For instance, over the Fourth of July holiday in 2011, Justin hung out with the godfather of hip-hop, Russell Simmons, on a yacht off the coast of Long Island. We know this because they tweeted pictures of each other "planking," a wacky Internet trend where you take a picture of yourself lying face down, hands at your side, straight as a board. Like a plank. The idea is to "plank" in the most random place possible. On top of a refrigerator. On a church pew. Or, in Justin's case, on the tail end of a really big yacht. He might be one of the most famous people on the planet, but Justin's still just a goofy kid.

Let's pray he stays that way as long as he possibly can.

Chapter 7

Never Say Never

Nothing, you see, is impossible with God.

— LUKE 1:37

One afternoon in March 2011, I heard the familiar creak of the front gate and a thud as my son dropped his backpack on the living room floor above me. I bounded up the stairs from my office, grabbed my car keys, and before he could reach for his Nintendo DS, announced, "Keep your shoes on; we're going to a movie."

It was a school day. We don't normally go see movies during the week, so he hustled out the front door (before I could change my mind) and climbed into the car. He didn't even ask which movie until I fastened my seatbelt and started to back out of the driveway.

"The Justin Bieber movie," I said.

"Oh," Vasco said, in a less-than-excited-but-happy-to-be-here kind of way.

"It's in 3D—at the IMAX," I explained. That got him.

The awesome stadium seats. Those funky, plastic 3D glasses. Sometimes the IMAX theater closest to our home in Southern

California even had its own portable refreshment stand inside the theater so you didn't have to go to the lobby to buy snacks.

Fifteen minutes later we arrived at the Cineplex, bought a huge tub of popcorn, drinks, a box of Raisinets for me and a bag of Twizzlers for him, scoped out two perfect seats (in the center, toward the back), unwrapped our special Bieber edition, purple 3D shades, and settled in a few minutes before the previews began.

"Is it real?" Vasco asked before the lights dimmed a little more, signaling that the feature film was about to begin. By "real" he meant, is it real like something we watch on the Discovery channel versus a "story" like *Star Wars* or Harry Potter.

"Yes, it's real. It's the real story of his life and concert tour," I told him.

"So, it's actually him?" he asked, looking a bit skeptical. "Not an actor?"

Nope. The real McCoy. The Crown Prince of Canada. The Biebs himself.

And as the film began, I leaned over, pointed at the screen and said, "And that's his mom."

Directed by Jon M. Chu (*Step Up 2: The Streets* and *Step Up 3D*), the film is part biography, part concert film and tells Justin's story from his childhood in Canada through his historic concert at New York City's Madison Square Garden on August 31, 2010. It focuses particular attention on the ten days leading up to Justin's show at the Garden as he prepares to play one of the most prestigious venues in the world, one that he famously sold out in twenty-two minutes.

The film has grossed more than $98 million worldwide since its release in February 2011, making it the No. 1 concert film of all time (unseating Michael Jackson's posthumous *This is*

It) and the No. 3 feature-length documentary of all time (behind *March of the Penguins* and Michael Moore's *Fahrenheit 9/11*).

> "Justin inspired me to play piano, and I play by ear. . . . He was a big influence on me to pursue piano playing. . . . The first song I learned to play was 'Baby' by Justin Bieber."
> — Camille, 14, Nashville, TN

Often funny and sometimes startlingly poignant, *Never Say Never* is a thoroughly enjoyable film. Justin is charming and his God-given musical talents shine. The bulk of the film is told in "behind the scenes" footage where we meet Pattie; Scooter; Kenny; Mama Jan; "swagger coach" Ryan; Justin's father, Jeremy; and grandparents, Bruce and Diane Dale; and we feel like we actually get to know most of them pretty well. They are an entertaining and loveable band of characters who collectively comprise Team Bieber.

There are baby pictures of Justin and video clips of him as a toddler banging on a kitchen chair, learning to play the drums and the guitar, playing soccer and hockey, singing at home and in the Stratford Idol contest, as well as footage of him in the studio and hanging out with celebrity friends such as his mentor, Usher, Jaden Smith, Ludacris, the fellas from Boyz II Men, Miley Cyrus, and Sean Kingston—all of whom recorded songs with him for his first two albums.

The strength of the film lies in Justin's story, which feels more like a fairy tale on the big screen than it does even in print. He works hard, plays hard, doesn't take himself too seriously, and has great faith. It is this last part that caught many viewers off guard. I don't think many fans understood just how genuine and central Justin's faith is or how deliberately his mother has tried to foster his love for God. Pattie comes across like a tiny

Canadian Queen Esther in stilettos and skinny jeans—heroic, steadfast, and ferociously protective of her child, for whom she is both an anchor of stability and a bottomless well of unconditional love.

I didn't have many preconceived notions or expectations about the film before we saw it. But I certainly didn't expect to be moved to tears—several times.

Justin is rough on his voice. The Energizer Bunny on steroids, he's forever shouting and horsing around, actually bouncing off of walls sometimes, and keeps going and going and going until he simply runs out of juice. "He's sixteen years old and doesn't know when to shut up," Mama Jan says after giving Justin, his voice in tatters, a bit of a dressing down backstage. A week before his concert at Madison Square Garden, which came halfway through his My World tour of North America's eighty-five performances, he caught a cold and his voice was shot. Doctors were called, Justin was ordered to go on total vocal rest (which meant no talking at all—not even whispering), and forced to postpone his show in Syracuse, New York, six days before the concert at the Garden, in the hopes that his voice would recover enough for him to perform. Justin truly hates to disappoint his fans and fought to keep the Syracuse show alive, but the choice was clear: play Syracuse, push his voice too far, and have to cancel a half dozen shows down the road or move the Syracuse show until later in the tour and hopefully carry on with the other dates as planned.

The night before the Madison Square Garden show Justin reaches a low point. He's sick, exhausted, frustrated, depressed, and not allowed to speak. My heart went out to him as he sat on the couch, silently sending out tweets to his fans who responded with thousands of messages of their own, encouraging him, trying to boost his spirits, telling him that they were praying for him. In one of the most moving scenes in the film, Pattie goes to her boy, who is lying in a heap on the bed in the back of his tour bus. Very quietly, in the dimly lit sleeping compartment, Pattie crawls onto the bed, puts her arms around Justin, holds his hand, and begins to pray.

"God, I pray that you would just make Justin's headache go away," she prayed softly. "We pray for complete healing."

> "I'm very glad that he's able to share his music with everybody and comfortable enough to share his faith and knowledge of his faith with the world. He's just awesome like that."
> —Hannah, 12, St. Louis, MO

Sitting with my own son in that theater, I was a puddle, and I know I'm not alone in how moved I was by that scene. Justin wasn't fighting for his life or in any great peril, but that didn't make the scene any less powerful. Every parent—every child, for that matter—has been in that moment, where there's brokenness and the need for healing, mercy, and grace. It was such a real, true moment and said more about Pattie and Justin's faith and relationship in a few seconds on film than they could have expressed in a million words.

Of course, Justin did recover his voice and his spirit in time to play the sold-out show in New York City. When he takes the stage for the first time, I had to stifle a cheer. If I were giving my "testimony," to use a religious term that describes when a person of faith shares their conversion story, that right there would be the moment I became a Belieber.

Throughout the film, Chu includes footage of Scooter, Ryan, and others from Team Bieber heading out into the crowds of fans gathered in the parking lots of stadiums, arenas, and theaters hours before Justin's concerts are set to begin. They give away free tickets—and good ones up front near the stage—to fans who don't have them. "Me and the guy from 'Extreme Home Makeover' have the best jobs in the world," Scooter says. "We get paid just to make people happy."

My favorite scene takes place outside Scotiabank Place in Ottawa, Canada. Ryan and another road manager, Alison Kaye, head out with a fistful of tickets. They come up to a group of four teenage girls and ask whether they have tickets. They don't. Are they big fans? Oh yeah.

"What's your favorite song?" Alison asks.

One of the girls, a beautiful teenager wearing a hijab—a head scarf often traditionally worn by observant Muslim girls and women—breaks into a soulful *a cappella* rendition of "That Should Be Me." When Ryan and Alison surprise the girls with tickets, they start screaming with joy, grab the tickets, and start running toward the entrance to the stadium.

> "It's amazing how people can just join in when you start talking about Justin. They may not even know much about him and they're like, 'Whoa! I never knew that before.' But Justin saying all that stuff [about faith], it's really cool because then they're able to learn the love of God themselves, like 'Oh! Maybe if I pray, then something will happen, like maybe I'll see a sign from God or something.' And then maybe they actually get a sign and find God. It's a really amazing thing." — Bridget, 16, Crystal Lake, IL

In the theater that afternoon in March, this scene once again brought me to tears. Vasco looked over at me and gave me that, "Are you crying?" look, like Tom Hanks does in that dugout scene from *A League of Their Own.*

"Are you okay, Mum?" he whispered.

"Oh yeah, I'm fine, honey," I croaked.

Why *was* I crying?

First of all, I saw myself in those girls. Back in the 1980s when I was their age, if Paul McGuinness and Sheila Roche from Team U2 had walked up to me outside the Meadowlands and handed me tickets to see my favorite band play, I would have had a heart attack. It would have been me screaming, "This is the best thing that's ever happened to me in my entire life!" with tears running down my face. But it's something more than that. It's about grace. As I understand it, grace is something God gives every single one of us, whether we realize, recognize it, or deny it, because God loves us. We can't earn it. We can't do anything to un-earn it, either. It's a gift—a free gift, a surprise, a little bit more, and the extra cherry on top of an ice cream sundae. Grace comes from God, but sometimes God uses us to show it to each other. And that's what Ryan and Alison did for those girls in Ottawa.

It also touched me deeply that the fan who sang so beautifully, the one that Alison and Ryan extended such a wonderful gift to, was a Muslim. Here's this Christian kid from Canada whose music this Muslim girl loves so much despite their cultural or religious differences, being blessed in a small but mighty way. She'll remember that moment for the rest of her life. And that, to me, is incredibly beautiful. That is what following Jesus is supposed to be all about. Loving people. Blessing them. No matter who they are.

Giving away concert tickets is part of Team Bieber's commitment to pay it forward to the fans who have given Justin this amazing life. As Vasco and I left the theater that day, I felt like Justin and his people had given us a gift. A surprise blessing we hadn't been expecting and that knocked the wind out of me with its beauty.

In the car on the way home, Vasco said he really liked the film and then got quiet for a moment. "Mum, do you think I could do that?" he asked.

"Do what, honey?" I said.

"You know, what Justin did. If you made a video of me singing and put it up on the Internet, do you think that could happen to me?"

It was my turn to get quiet.

I thought about how improbable this scenario was. Sitting next to me in the car was this boy who, two years before, was living on the street in Malawi, an AIDS orphan, all alone, dying of a heart defect he had at birth. And now he's here. With me. In California. Healthy and happy and full of life, hopes, and dreams. Not long ago, it seemed impossible. But it wasn't.

Trying my darnedest to hold back tears, I turned to my son—my son, my beautiful boy, the light of my life—and said, "Why not? Anything's possible."

Never say never.

JUSTIN
BY THE NUMBERS

(as of July 15, 2011)

- Number of followers on his official Twitter feed: 11,071,683

- Number of people he "follows" on his official Twitter page: 116,394

- Number of Tweets from @justinbieber on Twitter since March 2009: 9,961

- Number of followers on his official Facebook page: 33,069,451

- Number of subscribers to his official YouTube channel (kidrauhl): 1,276,679

- Number of channel views on his official YouTube channel: 73,897,980

- Number of uploaded video views on his official YouTube channel: 340,875,470

- Number of times the video of Justin singing Ne-Yo's "So Sick"—the first video posted to his YouTube account on January 19, 2007—has been viewed: 4,181,584

- Number of views of his video "Pray" on YouTube: 47,947,226

- Number of hits for the "Justin Bieber" search on Google: 490 million

- Day @justinbieber broke the 10 million followers threshold on Twitter: May 28, 2011

- Day @justinbieber broke the 11 million followers mark on Twitter: July 14, 2011

- Day @justinbieber is expected to surpass 20 million followers (according to Twittercounter.com) on Twitter: November 23, 2012

- Number of people who follow his mother, Pattie Mallette, on her official Twitter feed @studiomama: 608,103

- Number of people who follow his manager, Scooter Braun, on his official Twitter feed @scooterbraun: 892,135

- Number of people who follow his bodyguard, Kenny Hamilton, on his official Twitter feed @kennyhamilton: 487,035

- Number of albums sold: 6 million (according to figures from Soundscan)

- Box office revenue for his film *Never Say Never* worldwide: $98,441,954

- Box office revenue for *Never Say Never* in the United States: $73,013,910

- The minimum amount he makes per concert per night (according to TheSmokingGun.com): $300,000

- Estimated total box office gross from the first leg of his "My World" tour: $35.6 million

- Time it took him to sell out his show at Madison Square Garden in New York City (capacity about 20,000) in 2010: 22 minutes

- Time it took him to sell out more than 28,000 tickets to shows at the O2 Arena in Dublin, Ireland, in 2011: 10 minutes

11 million followers on Twitter is

- About 1/20 of the number of total users on Twitter

- More than twice as many followers as Justin Timberlake has on his official Twitter feed @jtimberlake

- About 2.5 million more followers than Britney Spears has on her official Twitter feed @britneyspears

- About 2 million more followers than U.S. President Barack Obama has on his official Twitter feed @barackobama

- About 600,000 fewer followers than Lady Gaga has on her official Twitter feed @ladygaga

- More than 367 times the population of his hometown Stratford, Ontario, in Canada

- 400,000 people more than the population of Los Angeles

- More than 1/3 the population of Canada (34 million)

- More than 3/4 of the population of Ontario (13 million)

- More than twice the populations of Latvia (2.2 million) and Lesotho (2.17 million) combined

- About twice the population of Denmark (5,564,219)

#killem
withkindness

A sense of humor is just common sense, dancing.

— WILLIAM JAMES

*Love your enemies. Let them bring out the best in you,
not the worst. When someone gives you a hard time,
respond with the energies of prayer, for then you are
working out of your true selves, your God-created selves.*

— MATTHEW 5:43

Justin has millions of passionately loyal fans around the globe.

He is one of the most recognizable people on the planet.

These two indisputable facts also, sadly, lead to a third: He has a lot of haters.

And they're organized. On Facebook, where Justin's official page had a stunning 33,069,451 fans as of July 15, 2011, there are hundreds of other pages where people who don't like him gather to share their contempt for the seventeen-year-old superstar. The largest of these pages—and most of them are named "I Hate Justin Bieber" or some variation of the same—had

1,854,378 fans. Sure, that's only a tiny fraction of Justin's Facebook fan base, but it's still a whole lot of people.

"There are always going to be people who don't like you and want to tear you down in life in general," Justin said. "I feel like it has to make you stronger. If you didn't have 'haterz' then you'd be doing something wrong. You have to have those people who don't like you . . . A lot of people don't like me because they don't know my story."

The "unBeliebers," we'll call them, don't just show up online. During the National Basketball Association All-Star Game at New York City's Madison Square Garden on February 2, 2011— the same venue where tickets for his 2010 concert sold out in twenty-two minutes—when Justin, who was sitting courtside, appeared on the Jumbotron briefly during a timeout, the crowd booed. Loudly and for more than just a few seconds.

> "From what I see of him, I find that he's really just *kind*.
> To everybody."   — Hannah, 12, St. Louis, MO

On YouTube, video clips of Justin's guest appearance in a 2010 episode of the television program *CSI: Crime Scene Investigation* where his character is shot to death have been viewed more than ten million times. I'm going to go out on a limb and say that not all of those ten million clicks were from Beliebers admiring his acting chops. And speaking of acting chops, months after Justin taped those *CSI* episodes, one of his co-stars on the show, the actress Marg Helgenberger, told a reporter that Justin was "a brat." (Beliebers were outraged—their wrath can be pretty fearsome—and Helgenberger has since retracted the remark.)

Justin's feelings were hurt and he tweeted about the incident,

Belieber!

ending with the tag #killemwithkindness. "Kill them with kindness" has become a mantra in the Bieber Nation for the best way to react to "haterz."

@justinbieber, May 9, 2011

> it's kinda lame when someone you met briefly and never worked with comments on you. I will continue to wish them luck and be kind. #killemwithkindness

> Even last week they had me scolded on a plane in the news because i wasnt in my seat fast enough. She was right and i sat down. That's news?

> I know who i am and sometimes people r just going 2 say what they want. Keep ur head up and be the man ur mama raised. #killemwithkindness

> u cant play 2 rumors. u cant let hate beat u down. u need 2 know who you r and kill them with kindness. take the high road - positive energy
> as for now...we are in the JUNGLE!! http://youtu.be/rSrqdqRM1Dg

@justinbieber, May 26, 2010

> i know my friends family and fans know the person i am. hearing adults spread lies and rumors is part of the job i guess. but all i have to say is...kill em with kindness.

> so everyone keep smiling...we r all blessed and I am still grateful and appreciate the opportunity u have all given me to do what i love

> just gonna chill...kill 'em with kindness

Rumors of Justin's (actual, rather than television) death have spread like wildfire—causing near mass hysteria on Twitter—on at least three separate occasions since 2009. Some of those rumors were reportedly staged by unBeliebers organized through the website 4Chan.com, where a number of super-successful Internet pranks have been hatched in recent years, including the phenomenon known as "Rickrolling" where Internet hyperlinks were disguised to lead to the video for '80s crooner Rick Astley's song "Never Gonna Give You Up" instead of their purported destination.

Justin is a legendary prankster with a great sense of humor, and his reaction to the occasional widespread rumors of his demise—by, variously, a bullet to the heart, a car wreck, suicide, and a "late-night altercation" in New York City—has been light-hearted. "I'm not dead. I had to check on this one . . . but it turns out I'm alive" was his response, via Twitter, to the bullet-to-the-heart rumor in the summer of 2011.

> "I was actually watching an interview on YouTube and he was talking about his biggest influence, and he said his mom, but then he also said that God and the Bible really keep him strong in the industry."
> — Camille, 14, Nashville, TN

Suffering through ridiculous rumors seems to be part of celebrity's package deal, and Justin has weathered more than a few doozies. Many of the most bizarre ones seem to be related to his high-pitched voice (before it changed in mid-2010), such as "Justin takes estrogen" and "Justin had his left testicle removed." Then there were the rumors about his "true" religious identity. "Justin is a Scientologist" and "Justin is a member of the Illuminati" being the most prevalent. (The Illuminati are allegedly members of a super-secret organization that controls world events behind the scenes.)

With characteristic good humor—"these are always fun!"— Justin took to Twitter on June 29, 2010, with a series of posts dispelling some of those "crazy rumors," beginning with a stubborn one alleging that his mom, Pattie, had been offered $50,000 to pose for *Playboy* Magazine. (Four days before her son tweeted his rumor-corrections, Pattie also reacted to the *Playboy* rumor

Belieber!

on Twitter, saying, "PLAYBOY!? Heavens No! . . . Thx but no thx! My son finds this rumor hysterical! Please don't believe what u read!")

@justinbieber, June 29, 2010

let's take some time to answer some crazy rumors....these are always fun...

my mom is a moral woman...let's just leave that one for what it is...because that rumor just grossed and wierded me out. . .

I have not joined the Illuminati or any other cult. Im a christian and I pray before every show and am thankful for every blessing

Im not Peter Pan...Im growing up and my voice will change but no worries Jan Smith is the greatest vocal coach ever...stronger than ever!

I am not the son of CHUCK NORRIS....although he did give birth to Hercules

I am not 10 feet tall and I dont shoot fire balls from my arse....that was Brave-Heart

@asherroth is not my real big bro...he is just the big bro in friendship...we have Bromance. haha

Im home schooled and not going to a high school next year in every city we have visited...

...although i would like to sit next to all u girls in math class ;)

and the truth is I LOVE MY FRIENDS, FAMILY, and MY FANS. Im the same kid I always was...there is just a lil more pressure. I luv all yall!!

In early 2011, around the same time he appeared on the covers of *Vanity Fair* and *Rolling Stone* magazines (covered by red lipstick kisses in the former and accompanied by the headline "Super Boy" in the latter), Justin (as a less-than-flattering cartoon version of himself) also graced the cover of *MAD*, the infamous satirical magazine. His friend, Miley Cyrus, dressed up as Justin and mocked him in a skit on *Saturday Night Live*, and his name is a popular punch line for late-night talk show opening monologues.

Justin seems to take such humorous jabs at his persona in stride, but sometimes the shade that gets thrown in his direction does cast a pall. Still, at least publicly, he seldom returns the snarkiness in kind, instead choosing to use his discomfort as a teachable moment for his fans. Via Twitter, he often tells his fans not to pay attention to rumors because he communicates with them directly in tweets and will always tell it like it is. And occasionally, his tweets take a spiritually serious turn, as they did on May 26, 2010, when Justin wrote, "I was raised to respect others and not gossip, nor answer gossip with anger."

> "To be that young and in the light, and to be like, 'I love Jesus,' that's huge in itself and he's getting tons of crap for it. And these people are going to be waiting to see him mess up, just to say, 'See? He's like every other pop star.' So far he's done a pretty good job of keeping that good reputation." — Carl, 20, Chicago, IL

It's not clear what prompted him to post an unusually lengthy and painfully honest series of tweets on January 19, 2011—he had traveled all day and was about to start mandatory vocal rest (which he hates)—but in a dozen tweets posted over the course of a half-hour in the middle of the night, Justin bared his heart, venting some frustrations but ending, as he does, with encouraging words—for his fans and himself.

Remember, kindness is always the best weapon.

@justinbieber, Jan. 19, 2011

> i think i understand im not living a normal life anymore...but im normal. people say all sorts of stuff but i know who i am and im grateful

and i know some dudes are gonna talk trash and others are gonna show love. thats life. i just love what i do. guess its that simple

and i love all of you showing me support in my dreams and sharing yours with me. and i also love taking a hater and proving them wrong

guess what im saying is do what u love and never let anyone stop u. stay true to yourself and dont judge a book by its cover. #respect

and im gonna prove all that in #NEVERSAYNEVER3D on FEBRUARY 11th.... @ jonmchu sorry that was a #shamelessplug haha

i had to...i had to...lol

#latenightventing

but 4 real we all get frustrated at times. we wanna show people who judge us so quick who we really are. sometimes u gotta just let it ride

cant win them all. just gotta be youself. all days arent fun but everyday is another opportunity. gotta be grateful for that

been fun rambling.

Chapter 9

Nobody's Perfect

If God only used perfect people, nothing would get done.
God will use anybody if you're available.

— Pastor Rick Warren, The Purpose-Driven Life

You'll watch over every step I take, but you won't keep
track of my missteps. My sins will be stuffed in a sack
and thrown into the sea—sunk in deep ocean.

— Job 14:1

A reporter once asked Pattie Mallette what her greatest challenge was in parenting Justin.

"He's so, so, SO strong willed," Pattie answered. "I thought *I* was strong willed. I have to stay consistent and stay on it when I decide on something and not back down because he is so strong willed.

"I think it's such a great quality," she continued. "I know there are other kids out there who are so strong willed and their parents don't know what to do with them because they're not like that and their other kids aren't like that. But those are the kids who make really strong leaders."

What's the worst thing Justin's ever done?

"He snuck out one night to go bike riding with a friend at, like, two in the morning and got brought home by police," Pattie said. "He really wasn't doing anything. I think it was good for him because it scared him so much that he didn't want to take that chance again."

That was Pattie's answer in 2009, when Justin was fifteen and standing on the verge of superstardom. I wonder whether her answer would be different now.

The kind of celebrity that Justin has achieved has many blessings: financial prosperity, a rarified kind of influence on the world, privilege and access to experiences and people—President Obama has his cell phone number—which the rest of us only dream about. But there are drawbacks to Justin's fame as well. His life as a private person ended when he was fourteen. He's followed everywhere he goes by paparazzi, their cameras and videophones pointed at him, waiting for him to make a mistake.

Whether he likes it or not, Justin is a role model for millions of young people around the world. It's a position he takes very seriously, while admitting that it is a substantial burden. "It's definitely a big responsibility," Justin said. "So I always have to make sure I make the right decisions. A lot of times I'm going to make mistakes, but I'm human. I do the best I can. I try to be a good role model. That's all."

Can you imagine living with the kind of public scrutiny that Justin does, in the glare of the harshest of spotlights? If the paparazzi had followed me around when I was a teenager, I'm sure the video clips would have horrified me. And I was a good kid. I didn't drink or smoke or do drugs or hang out with people who did, but I was still a kid with raging hormones, mood swings, and a big personality. Often I didn't think before

Belieber: Fame, Faith and the Heart of Justin Beiber

Justin's meteoric rise to fame is often described as a real-life Cinderella (or Cinder*fella*) story. Plucked from obscurity in his native Canada, Justin quickly has become one of the most recognized people in the world and the "most popular teen-ager" on the planet. Here are a selection of snapshots from Justin's journey of fame (and faith), from his childhood in Stratford, Ontario, to the world stage.

Canada and the United States

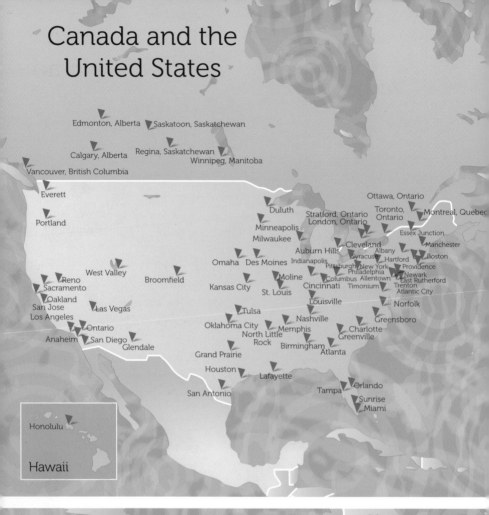

Edmonton, Alberta
Saskatoon, Saskatchewan
Calgary, Alberta
Regina, Saskatchewan
Winnipeg, Manitoba
Vancouver, British Columbia
Everett
Portland

Ottawa, Ontario
Toronto, Ontario
Montreal, Quebec
Duluth
Stratford, Ontario
London, Ontario
Essex Junction
Minneapolis
Milwaukee
Cleveland
Manchester
Albany
Auburn Hills
Syracuse
Hartford
Boston
Omaha
Des Moines
Indianapolis
Pittsburgh
New York
Providence
West Valley
Moline
Columbus
Philadelphia
Newark
Reno
Cincinnati
Allentown
East Rutherford
Sacramento
Broomfield
Kansas City
Timonium
Trenton
Oakland
St. Louis
Atlantic City
San Jose
Las Vegas
Louisville
Norfolk
Los Angeles
Tulsa
Greensboro
Ontario
Nashville
Anaheim
San Diego
Oklahoma City
Memphis
Charlotte
Glendale
North Little
Greenville
Rock
Birmingham
Atlanta
Grand Prairie
Houston
Lafayette
San Antonio
Tampa
Orlando
Sunrise
Miami

Honolulu

Hawaii

Australia

Perth
Brisbane
Adelaide
Sydney
Melbourne

Europe and Israel

Newcastle, England ▼
Liverpool, England ▼
Sheffield, England ▼
Manchester, England ▼
Nottingham, England ▼
Dublin, Ireland ▼
Birmingham, England ▼
London, England ▼
Herning, Denmark ▼
Berlin, Germany ▼
Oberhausen, Germany ▼
Rotterdam, The Netherlands ▼
Antwerp, Belgium ▼
Paris, France ▼
Zurich, Switzerland ▼
Milan, Italy ▼
Barcelona, Spain ▼
Madrid, Spain ▼
Tel Aviv, Israel ▼

East Asia

Tokyo, Japan ▼
Osaka, Japan
Taipei, Taiwan ▼
Hong Kong, China ▼
Manila, Philippines ▼
Kuala Lampur, Malaysia ▼
Singapore ▼
Bogor, Indonesia ▼

Justin Bieber performs
at the ACC in Toronto
on Aug. 21, 2010.

Justin's best friends, Chaz Somers (L) and Ryan "Butsy" Butler (R), riding bikes through the streets of their hometown, Stratford, Ontario.

©2011, Toronto Star

Justin gets a kiss from his great-grandmother, Estelle Corbeil, at a Feb. 1, 2011 screening of *Never Say Never* in Toronto, Canada.

Justin's stepsister, Jazmyn Bieber, plays with a cutout of her big brother on the purple carpet of the Toronto premiere of his film, *Never Say Never*, Feb. 1, 2011.

Justin with girlfriend Selena Gomez
at the 2011 MuchMusic Award.

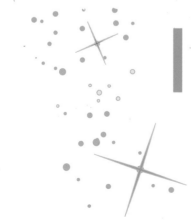

Justin walks with manager Scooter
Braun (right) while carrying
stepsister Jazmyn Bieber during a
visit to Toronto in February 2011.

Justin Bieber greets screaming fans at the MuchMusic Environment in Toronto, Canada, Aug. 7, 2009.

(L-R) Justin's stepsister Jazmyn, father Jeremy Bieber, Justin, and mother, Pattie Mallette at a Feb. 1, 2011 Toronto screening of his film, *Never Say Never*.

Rene Johnston/Toronto Star ©2011, Toronto Star

Justin Bieber plays the packed Air Canada Center on Nov. 23, 2010 after winning at the American Music Awards.

JUSTIN BIEBER

©2011, Toronto Star

Justin Bieber is greeted by Toronto rapper Drake, Feb. 1, 2011.

Justin at a press conference in Toronto, Canada, Feb. 1, 2011 with road manager Alison Kaye (R).

Justin Bieber, seen playing the Kool Haus, Nov. 6, 2009.

(L-R) Usher, Justin, and Scooter Braun attend the *Justin Bieber: Never Say Never* Los Angeles Premiere held at Nokia Theatre L.A. Live on Feb. 8, 2011.

Justin Bieber greets fans at the MuchMusic Video Awards in Toronto on June 20, 2010. His bodyguard, Kenny Hamilton, is pictured right, facing Justin and wearing dark glasses.

Justin Bieber shares a moment with his grandfather,
Bruce Dale, Nov. 6, 2009.

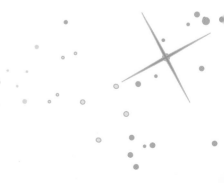

opening my mouth to speak, and made a few poor choices along the way that I would not want to watch on the evening news (or see posted on TMZ.com).

Like Justin, I committed my life to Jesus Christ at an early age and have had a personal relationship with him since I was in grade school. That means both of us made and will continue to commit our most spectacular mistakes and sins after the fact, which makes our conversion stories a lot more messy—and all the more embarrassing. When we screw up, there's that voice (sometimes external but usually in our own minds) that says, "Uh, aren't you supposed to know better? You *are* a Christian, after all."

Justin's manager, Scooter Braun, who just turned thirty, understands what it's like to navigate the strange new world of adulthood as a person of faith, with all of the joys, perils, and pitfalls that it entails.

"There's going to be mistakes I'm sure [he'll] make as a young man, like we all make," Scooter said. "But overall he has a really good heart and he's a very intelligent kid . . . For him it's about living his life to be the best example he can be for others."

As Justin transitions into young adulthood, he's going to make some decisions that he'll regret. We all do. How he handles those mistakes is what's really important. Will he self-correct, apologize, and make amends? Or will he make excuses for his behavior, refuse wise counsel, and continue to make lousy decisions that will lead him down a slippery slope, as so many child stars before him sadly have? A lot of people expect him to end up following in the footsteps of young celebrities such as Britney Spears, Aaron Carter, Jessica and Ashlee Simpson, and Miley Cyrus—all of whom share a similar spiritual background to Justin's.

According to a March 2011 poll by *60 Minutes/Vanity Fair*, 30 percent of Americans believe Justin will be in celebrity rehab when he reaches the age of thirty, and 18 percent of the 11,000 people surveyed for the poll said they thought that, by 2024, Justin would be married and living quietly somewhere away from the celebrity spotlight.

First of all, how mortifying is it that Justin would even be the subject of that kind of a survey? Second, if any young star is prepared to successfully avoid the "traps and snares," to use some biblical imagery, of celebrity, it's Justin. His mother and his management—led by Scooter and his mentor, Usher—have been extremely deliberate about surrounding Justin with good people who will keep him grounded and make sure his moral compass is working correctly. And Justin himself is all too aware of the dangers that many young celebrities have faced before him because he studies them.

In Justin's film, *Never Say Never*, Scooter recalls sitting with Justin in the audience of the MTV Video Music Awards in September 2009 as Madonna eulogized Michael Jackson. Justin is a massive fan of the "King of Pop" and had been pretty devastated by his sudden demise a few months earlier. When Madonna talked about Jackson's "lost childhood," Justin looked right at Scooter and said, "Don't let that happen to me."

Scooter, Pattie, and the rest of Justin's family are determined to do everything they can to make sure it doesn't. But in the final analysis, the choice is up to Justin. So far, he's avoided any disastrous choices (that we know of publicly), but since his seventeenth birthday in March 2011, there have been a few . . . well, let's call them *hiccups*.

Actually, the hiccupping started *on* his seventeenth birthday. Justin had celebrated over dinner at a Los Angeles restaurant with his girlfriend, Selena Gomez. (Hey, no hissing, Beliebers! She seems like a loving young lady. Be kind.) As they were leaving the restaurant, paparazzi—out in force—blocked their car and, as Selena shielded her face from the camera flashes, Justin gave the paps the finger. Of course, the whole incident was caught on camera and soon pictures of Justin flipping the bird were transmitted around the globe. Many fans were shocked, others cheered him on, believing the paparazzi deserved the obscene hand gesture. On Twitter, you would have thought Armageddon was underway.

> "I think he really cares about his fans, and when he makes a mistake, he feels awful about it. . . . People who have the courage to do that, they're the real role models, because they don't say, 'Well, I was upset,' or 'You can't blame me.' He really does feel bad about it."
> —Bridget, 16, Cyrstal Lake, IL

Justin quickly apologized, both to the photographers he'd insulted and to his fans, who, he said, rightly expect him to behave better than that. "I'm sorry . . . #killemwithkindness," he tweeted. "It's not always easy but I know better than to react in anger."

A month later in Tel Aviv, Israel, he had another run-in with the paparazzi while he was touring sacred sites with his family a few days before his concert there. The paps were so relentless, they even followed him into a church where he was trying to pray in peace. While he kept his hands in his pockets this time, Justin did vent his frustration with the paps on Twitter and then, acting like the crabby teenager he, in fact, was, threatened to spend the rest of his Israeli visit in his hotel room. Once again, after he cooled off for a few hours, Justin apologized via Twitter for losing his cool, saying that only some of the paparazzi had

been aggressive and that he was grateful to be in the Holy Land—
a pilgrimage that held profound meaning for him spiritually.

A few weeks after that, Justin's tour took him to Australia.
On a Qantas Airlines flight from Sydney to Melbourne, a flight
attendant chastised Justin for leaving his seat while the plane
was taxiing toward the runway. He apologized and took his seat.

No biggie, right?

> "If I could say anything to JB, I would probably say, 'Stay strong'—
> because he is in a world of people who live 'in the world' and are
> 'of the world.' And I would probably say, 'Keep believing.'"
> — Camille, 14, Nashville, TN

Wrong. The story was reported as front-page news in some
locations and was picked up by newspapers, television, and
online media outlets worldwide.

At the time, Justin said nothing publicly, but a few days
later, when *CSI* star Marg Helgenberger told a reporter that he
was "a brat" on the set, Justin piped up on Twitter, complain-
ing about gossip, rumors, and people generally being mean to
him. "Last week they had me scolded on a plane in the news
because I wasn't in my seat fast enough. She was right and I sat
down. That's news?" It probably shouldn't have made news but
Justin didn't do himself any favors by resurrecting the incident
publicly.

Justin is a strong-willed child and does have a temper. I can
relate—I am also strong willed as is my son. Considering the
kind of pressure Justin is under, I'm surprised it doesn't flare up
more often. To his credit, the vast majority of the time he keeps
it in check and is polite, kind, and generous to both his fans
and the media. (Even as a veteran of hundreds of interviews,

he still is known to occasionally hug reporters.) His schedule is grueling—he played more than a hundred concerts in less than a year. Some crankiness is to be expected, even from extraordinary souls.

After wrapping up his world tour in Japan in late May 2011, Justin took a vacation in Hawaii with his mother, Selena, and her parents. While it was obvious he and Selena had been dating for quite some time—despite coyly refusing to confirm their relationship publicly—they had always been very discreet. A few photos of them exchanging a quick peck on the lips were the only photographic evidence of their romance. Until that fateful day on the beach in Waikiki in June 2011.

A slew of photos surfaced on the Internet of Justin, shirtless in swimming trunks, and Selena, in a teeny bikini, making out. The images were pretty graphic, scandalizing many of his fans and leading many to speculate about whether the couple, who individually had made statements in the past about saving themselves for marriage, had, in fact, slept together. (Of course, the photos also gave rise in the weeks that followed to rumors that Selena was pregnant, though there is no evidence to support such claims.)

I have to admit that, as a mom, the Hawaiian pictures made me cringe and worry about "the lad," as I have come to think of him. Justin is seventeen and Selena is eighteen, almost exactly the same age as Justin's parents were when he was conceived. I was not alone in my concern for the young couple and the decisions they might be making.

"Of course I'm worried, even with a chaperone. I'm a mama!" Pattie said in an uncharacteristically revealing tweet. (Apparently, she wasn't there the day the photos were taken.)

I'm sure Pattie was praying like the fierce spiritual warrior she is. Justin is becoming a young man and the only person who can control his behavior is him. But that didn't stop me and many other fans from praying for him, that God would protect him, help him make wise decisions, and guard his heart. I was reminded of Pattie's prayer request list and the urgency she feels about covering her son in prayer. There are many people who regularly pray for my child as I do for theirs. Prayer is powerful.

Justin should always remember that with the many blessings God has bestowed on him comes great responsibility. He is sometimes painfully aware that his behavior—good or bad—sets an example for millions of fans around the globe, and I know he hates to disappoint them. That said, we—those of us who watch him from a safe distance—should be careful not to try to make him into some sort of Christian superhero. He is just as imperfect and vulnerable as the rest of us. The only difference is that his starlight shines a bit brighter than most of ours. He will not and could not be perfect. Justin would likely be among the first to say that, while he loves and appreciates his fans, for true believers, the only celebrity whose way of life we should worry about comparing ourselves to is Jesus.

Celebrity is big business and celebrity-toppling is practically a national sport. As a culture, we place celebrities on pedestals and then take great delight in knocking them off. We lift our pointy lances of judgment at the famous and infamous alike, feeling somehow self-satisfied when they fall. By the same token, though, we Americans in particular love nothing more than a good comeback story. When the glitterati stumble and descend into scandal or heartache, we cheer them on when they climb back up on their own two feet and once again ascend the pedestal. And the cycle repeats.

How we respond to or judge a superstar on his or her worst day says more about us than it does about them. Nothing brings out our bloodlust like a whiff of hypocrisy. For celebrities who have associated themselves with one religious tradition or another, or who have made statements about their faith and how it affects the way they live their lives—their ideas of what's right and what's wrong, what they will and won't do—making choices that seem to fly in the face of their previous spiritual statements is like waving huckleberries at a hungry bear. Our fangs come out when we see someone talking the talk but not walking the walk. Yet we all are hypocrites, when we stop to think about it. We all are guilty of saying we believe one thing and then behaving in a polar opposite way. In a sense, we're all moral acrobats. So why do we react to a celebrity's hypocrisy—real or perceived—with so much hostility?

As Justin continues his journey—with the ups and downs, joys and failures, and unexpected detours that surely will come—may we support him in prayer, be gentle and kind to him when he stumbles, and remember that God never runs out of patience for his children and that grace makes brokenness beautiful.

"Point your kids in the right direction—when they're old they won't be lost" (Proverbs 22:6).

Chapter 10

Voice of a Generation

Preach the gospel always, and if necessary, use words.

— ST. FRANCIS OF ASSISSI

God doesn't want us to be shy with his gifts,
but bold and loving and sensible.

— 2 TIMOTHY 1:5

I have a confession to make.

Before I started working on this book, I don't believe I had heard a single one of Justin's songs—at least not intentionally. I certainly knew his name, thanks in large part to PerezHilton .com, a regular stop on my daily tour of Internet news sites.

From Perez I knew that Justin was

1. Canadian
2. a teenager
3. a friend of Usher, and
4. cute as a button

The first time I heard Justin's voice was during his April 10, 2010, guest appearance on *Saturday Night Live,* in the skit where he played "Jason," a high school student in a class taught by the show's host, Tina Fey.

"I bet these tests were a pain to grade," Justin said. "Hope you didn't lose your whole evening. Oh well, back to learning."

Tina stared back at Justin adoringly and the audience heard her internal monologue in a voiceover: "Now see? That young man makes me feel like I'm doing a good job. Plus, his smile is like watching a baby bunny sniff a tiny flower."

This next part is painful for me to admit, but here it goes: The first song I heard Justin *sing* was the goofy spoof "Baby Lady" that ended the skit.

I'll buy you a panini
And some Spanx to make you teeny
You're the lady with the big brown eyes

And then . . . I changed the channel before Justin could perform "Baby" on SNL's fabled Studio 8H stage.

I *know*. I'm sorry.

Not quite a year later, my eleven-year-old son, Vasco, came home from school one afternoon and asked, "Mum, who is Jason Beaver?" (Vasco spent the first nine years of his life in Africa and has only been speaking English for a couple of years, so that might explain his difficulty with Justin's actual name.)

"JUSTIN, honey. Justin BIEBER," I said. "He's a singer. Why do you ask?"

"All the girls, they like him, but the boys—they don't," he said. "Do I have any Justin Bieber on my iTouch?"

He didn't and when I asked if he would like me to download some of Justin's music from iTunes for him, Vasco said politely, "No, that's okay. But what about the Black Eyed Peas?"

That was the end of the conversation and Justin didn't cross my mind again until a few weeks later when I noticed the cover story of the February 2011 edition of *Rolling Stone* magazine: "The Adventures of Super Boy: God, girls and boatloads of swag."

It was the "God" part that piqued my interest.

The lengthy story was based on conversations *Rolling Stone* reporter Vanessa Grigoriadis had with Justin in Atlanta over several days in the winter of 2011 as he prepared for the release of his film, *Never Say Never*. Grigoriadis recounted the details of Justin's early life and how Scooter discovered him, which I'd never heard before and found terribly compelling. But what really made an impression on me was the way he responded to the reporter's questions related to his faith and beliefs.

Justin answered those questions with a refreshingly graceful blend of honesty, boldness, and humility that is rare for any celebrity, never mind an international superstar barely old enough to shave.

It wasn't so much *what* he said as *how* he said it.

Bieber is a heartfelt Christian, but he's nervous talking about it, and makes sure that I'm a Christian too before he opens up. He says that if he could be one character from the Bible, he would choose Job, because he lost everything and stayed faithful to God. He also believes in angels, and thinks he might have been touched by one once, in the form of a kid at Christian camp who gave him a "really good-smelling" sweater and then disappeared, never to be seen again. "I feel that I have an obligation to plant little seeds with my fans," he says. "I'm not going to tell them, 'You need Jesus,' but I will say at the end of my show, 'God loves you.'"

He also says that he's going to heaven. "It says in the Bible that you go to heaven as long as you have God in your heart and ask for forgiveness of your sins," he says, with a smile that could warm the coldest heart.

He's definitely against abortion, too. "I really don't believe in abortion," he says. "I think [an embryo] is a human. It's like killing a baby." Even in the case of rape? "Um," he says. "Well, I think that's just really sad, but everything happens for a reason. I don't know how that would be a reason." He looks confused. "I guess I haven't been in that position, so I wouldn't be able to judge that."

To my ear at least, Justin didn't sound robotic or calculating, as if he were merely parroting back carefully rehearsed responses prepared by his management team or repeating what his mother had taught him to believe. They reflected a nonjudgmental, welcoming, love-forward face of a humble Christian believer.

His answers to difficult questions weren't caged or reticent. (And by the way, it takes some chutzpah on the reporter's part to ask a sixteen-year-old kid whose mother was eighteen and unmarried when he was born about abortion, knowing that if Pattie had chosen to handle her unplanned pregnancy differently Justin wouldn't even be here to answer.) But he is concerned about how what he says will affect other people, people who don't believe the same things he does. That, to me, is admirable. He doesn't appear to be concerned with being right, rather with being kind. That's a *loving* concern. And wasn't it Jesus himself who said people would know who his followers were because of their love?

♥ ♥ ♥

Justin's comments in *Rolling Stone* felt genuinely authentic and, now that I've read all of his more than 10,000 tweets and Facebook posts, true to form. (He either has the world's finest team of ghost writers or it really *is* him tweeting his frustration with the paparazzi at 3 a.m. from Israel, talking trash about his friend Adam Levine's basketball skills, telling his father how much he misses him and can't wait for Jeremy to join him on tour, or worrying about what he's going to wash his face with when he runs out of Proactiv on the road.)

> "I guess I'd want to ask him, 'Why do you believe in God the way that you do?'"
> — Riley, 9, Norwalk, CT

Justin is easily among the most prolific celebrity authors on Twitter. During the many months I spent researching this book, I followed Justin's tweets religiously (pardon the pun) and felt as if I'd gotten to know him pretty well 140 characters at a time. I could practically chart his movements and mood swings by reading his copious tweets. Justin willingly opens that window into his world and shares his day-to-day life with millions of fans. I knew where he was going, what he was doing, how he was feeling, and occasionally what he had for lunch.

On Twitter, his fans know, in real time, what's happening in Justin's world.

If he catches a cold, they know.

If he's just bested Scooter on the basketball court, they know.

If he's gone fishing with Kenny, they know.

If he's praying for a sick friend, someone touched by tragedy, or a nation suffering from the aftermath of a disaster (natural or otherwise), they know.

If he's written a new song he's excited about, they know.

If he's just watched *Talladega Nights: The Legend of Ricky Bobby* for the umpteenth time, they know.

If he's in a bad mood, boy, do they know.

If he needs to take a break from the limelight for a few days to spend some private time with his friends or family, they know.

Because he tells them.

Justin's generous transparency with his fans via Twitter is simply unprecedented for a celebrity. And he doesn't just allow his fans to be voyeurs, he communicates with them directly, reading their tweets, responding to questions and comments, offering prayers and support when they are struggling, and listening to their opinions and advice about what he should do next. He has more than eleven million followers on Twitter and it would be nearly impossible for him to "follow" all of them back. But he does make an effort to do so, following more than 100,000 fans, including me.

When someone follows you on Twitter, it allows you to send private messages to them directly. This is the Holy Grail of Bieber fandom. Millions of Beliebers spend hours posting tweets begging (or sometimes daring) Justin to follow them back so that they can have an even more intimate, direct connection to their hero. (I've direct messaged Justin a number of times, but alas, no response . . . yet.) How Justin came to follow my Twitter account is a complete mystery to me. Most fans know the precise date and time when Justin "followed them back." I didn't realize he had followed me until it was too late to go back in my Twitter feed's archive to establish the exact moment. (Fans lucky enough to be followed by Justin usually begin their short Twitter profile biographies with the date and time of the blessed event.) I actually feel guilty not knowing that critical Belieber information. And I'd love to know what made him choose @godgrrl from among the millions of other Twitter users that follow him. I guess I'll take a cue from Justin and just be grateful that he did.

> "My faith is renewed whenever I see a child with so much faith and belief in God who is willing to shout it out to the masses. Justin is such a kid and he has expressed his feelings about his belief many times here on YouTube. I see hope for the world, knowing that there are children like him for our future." — Randy via YouTube.com

The way Justin uses social media and new technology to create and maintain relationships with his fans (and friends) is emblematic of the way in which his generation views and engages with the world. Some older folks grouse about the way in which new-fangled gizmos such as cell phones, text messaging, laptops, iChat, Facebook, and Twitter have eroded what they call "real" relationships, by which they mean face-to-face or at least over a land line. People Justin's age just scratch their heads and continue connecting with friends and loved ones through their computer/phone/iPad screens. Technology is alienating people from one another, critics argue, and it provides a false sense of intimacy and connection. No one talks to each other any more, they grumble.

"Huh?" the Justin generation says. "Oh, sorry. Could you repeat that, please? I was distracted. My grandmother in Barcelona just FaceTimed me on my iPhone."

❤ ❤ ❤

When director Jon M. Chu set out to tell Justin's story in his documentary film—which, of course, famously opens with a shot of a computer monitor where someone is checking their email messages—it was clear that faith, hope, and charity would have to be central themes because they are the very things that define the arc of his young life. Justin's spiritual life—and that of his steadfast mother's—is a large part of what makes his story unique. That's not to say that there aren't other believers in the entertainment industry. They are, in fact, legion, but many celebrities shy away from wearing their religious beliefs on their sleeves lest they alienate part of their audience. In the world of celebrity, image is everything and most celebrities are careful to tailor theirs to appeal to as wide a swath of society as possible. That concept goes doubly for young would-be stars, most of whom are more carefully constructed and packaged than a pair of glass slippers.

For generations, the Hollywood industrial complex has churned out pop stars—sugary sweet or calculatingly alluring (and sometimes both), but always polished to perfection. On the surface, at least. Tinseltown is sadly littered with rags-to-riches-to-rags stories of stars whose childhood and innocence were mortgaged to buy fame and fortune, only to end up bankrupt in more ways than one when they approach adulthood and lose their cuteness quotient. From the young Frank Sinatra who nearly disappeared into obscurity when he crossed the threshold from teen idol to true adulthood, to Bobby Sherman, Bobby Driscoll, Danny Bonaduce, Mackenzie Phillips, Willie Aames, Tatum O'Neal, Leif Garrett, the Coreys (Haim and Feldman), or the child stars of *Diff'rent Strokes*, there are more cautionary tales than lifelong success stories in the annals of child celebrity.

Why should anyone expect a different outcome from the Biebs? Many people don't. But I do. The main reason for my optimism about what Justin's future might hold can be summed up in a single word: authenticity. Justin did not set out to find celebrity. He wasn't a prefabricated product manufactured by Disney or Nickelodeon. Nor is he a celebrity scion whose family provided him with a leg up in showbiz by virtue of his birthright. Fame and fortune found Justin, not the other way around, and because of that, worldly success does not appear to be the motivation behind what he does. God gave him gifts and the opportunity to use them. Justin rose to the occasion and worked hard to get where he is today. He still works hard and doesn't seem to take his success and all that comes with it for granted.

It is precisely that authenticity—his realness—humility and gratitude that appeals to his fans. And in turn, they feel a kinship with him that leads to fierce loyalty, a sense of ownership, and a passionate compulsion to protect and defend him as if he were one of their real-life friends. They love his music, his hair, his smile, and his dance moves, but they *know* his story on a soul level. Justin's young fans understood what he was all about long before the music critics and we media creatures had a clue. From his earliest days with a few hundred hits on YouTube, Justin's young fans resonated with his story and shared it with their friends. And then they walked with him into superstardom. Actually, they're the ones who carried him to it. It's a fact that Justin is ever aware of and thankful for. Rarely a day goes by when he doesn't express his gratitude to his fans—and God— on Twitter for blessing him with the extraordinary journey he's had since 2009. His fans love him. And he genuinely loves them back. For real.

I suppose that's another reason why I believe Justin's future is a bright one. He has the exceedingly rare gift of perspective. Even as a teenager, he is able to pan out and look at the big picture of his life story and realize the power it has to inspire people and point them toward its author: God.

"I think that it's important that people . . . see my story because it gives people hope," he said. "It's great for people to see that anything's possible. If you just focus and keep your dreams in front of you, never give up—never say never—then anything is possible."

> "One of the questions I've been thinking through in my head is: If God loves us so much, then why does he make us hurt so bad?"
> —Hannah, 12, St. Louis, MO

That same perspective also makes Justin aware that many people will dismiss him out of hand simply because of his age. "It's weird that people think I don't have a story because I'm so young," he said. "But I came from a small town. My parents split up basically when I was born. I lived with not a lot of money. People don't realize that young people can have stories and still have emotions and feelings and stuff. It doesn't make sense when people try to take that away from you."

Justin's fans not only want to know his story, they get it. They pay attention to what he's trying to accomplish in the world, through his art and his faith, and they take it seriously.

"He's a hard worker and I like that," said diehard Belieber Yaphet, twenty, an economics major at Wheaton College in Illinois, whose family emigrated from Ethiopia to the United States when he was a child. "He didn't have that much and neither did I. But he worked really hard and he used what he had. That, for me, resonates a lot."

Yaphet isn't exactly who comes to mind when most people hear the word "Belieber." Twelve-year-old girls with braces and purple sneakers, shrieking about how they're going to marry him some day? Yes. Absolutely. An African immigrant three years Justin's senior, who's studying at one of the preeminent Christian colleges in the world? Notsomuch.

But there are more Yaphets out there than you might imagine. They are fans of his music and his faith, who believe there's a lot more to the impact Justin is making on the world than what can be measured on the Billboard charts.

Like Justin, Yaphet is a born-again Christian. He's intrigued by the way Justin expresses his faith and would love to be able to dig deeper. "I'd love to ask him what his core values are," Yaphet said. "What does he really hold to? What are the nonnegotiables? As he makes decisions and comes to a fork in the road, what drives his decisions?"

Twenty-one-year-old Emily, who hails from Katy, Texas, recently graduated from Wheaton with a degree in interpersonal communications and Bible/theology. She, too, is a loyal Belieber, who finds Justin's faith compelling and is fascinated by how he will continue to express it in the public square. "By nature of him being a pop star and as big as he is, he sort of has a prophetic voice for this generation," she said. "And so by his being so vocal about not only his faith but moral and political issues like abortion, he's opening up this freedom for pre-teens and teenagers to feel comfortable saying, 'Yeah, I believe in Jesus and that's okay.' That's one thing that I think is great. You know, kids that might be shy or are ashamed of it, or don't want to talk about it, well Justin Bieber's talking about it, so it's cool."

If you visit his Tumblr blog called *di-'dak-tik*, you will find Jeremy, a Wheaton junior from suburban Detroit, writing about under-the-radar musicians and indie bands such as tUnE-yArDs, The Ambassadors, Paper Diamond, or The Cataracs. You probably won't find Jeremy, an international relations major, blogging about Justin's latest single. But that doesn't mean that he hasn't been following the Bieb's story.

He has—with a decidedly astute eye.

"I think Bieber is truly homemade, which I think makes him way more appealing," Jeremy said. "What's also interesting about him is that his music is, like, innocent in a time when so much of what's on the radio is filled with sexual innuendo. It's dirty and it's crass. It's refreshing to hear somebody like Justin, who's not a product of Disney or Nickelodeon, who just has a kind of wholesome package. And it's good to know that there are real values behind that . . . So I really appreciate that about him. The thing is, too, he's actually got swag. I mean, he's actually very, very cool. I remember seeing the film, and there's that scene where he's [backstage] preparing to go on and you see like Drake and Snoop and Kobe Bryant and all these people. I was like, 'Why the heck is Kobe Bryant at a Justin Bieber concert?'

> "He's definitely saying that, basically, anybody can love God. You don't have to keep him in your back pocket and then bring him out when you need him."   —Bridget, 16, Crystal Lake, IL

"But Justin, while having this mainstream kind of feel, he's actually got some distinctiveness to his character and he's cool and he can shoot the breeze with Drake and share the stage with Snoop," he said. While Justin has obvious cred in the hip-hop community, Jeremy wonders whether the same will be true of the Christian community.

"I feel like Christians sort of get this mind-set, that they find out that a celebrity is a Christian and they want to claim it, like, 'Oh, he's on *our* team!'" Jeremy said. "Even in saying those things I think it's pretty ironic that when somebody does fall, Christians step away or demonize that person—like Amy Grant or Sandi Patty, these types of people. So I would inquire to the Christian community, as this stuff's coming out about Justin, how can we embody grace toward him? Can we pray for Justin?

Can we, when he flips somebody off, can we kind of defend him as relates to his humanity and fallenness? I'd like to ask him how he feels about the Christian communities. 'Have they been supportive to you? Or are they just admiring you from afar?' "

It may not matter whether the Christian community ever fully embraces (or tries to co-opt) Justin and his story or not. I think his audience is much grander than any single religious demographic. His appeal transcends racial and cultural barriers as much as his music doesn't adhere to one distinct musical genre. Justin has worked with hip-hop and rap artists, R&B and pop stars, and beyond. (I mean, the lad won a country music award in 2011 for goodness sake.)

Justin is coming up in a new paradigm—musically, culturally, religiously. People his age aren't bound by the same definitions and divisions of the generations that have come before them. They're less likely to consider themselves "religious" but just as likely as their parents or grandparents to say that faith (or spirituality, to use a more popular word) is important and formative in their lives, even if they don't self-apply a denominational label or frequent a house of worship with any regularity. They're still seeking an authentic connection with God—whom the vast majority believes exists. Many also believe in life after death, heaven and hell, angels, and even in miracles. How they express their beliefs and spiritual search, however, has changed.

Several years ago, when I was a religion reporter for the Chicago *Sun-Times* newspaper, I had a conversation with Bill Hybels, cofounder of Willow Creek Community Church outside Chicago, one of the earliest and most successful evangelical mega-churches in the United States, on the occasion of Willow's thirtieth anniversary. I asked Bill whether what people are searching for spiritually had changed much in thirty years. His answer is something I think about often, even years later, and I believe it speaks to the heart of Justin's unprecedented popularity worldwide.

"Thirty years ago, we argued about what was true," Bill told me. "These days people seem to be asking, what's real?"

Real. Genuine. Authentic.

Justin's loyal fans may be drawn to him at first because, to quote Tina Fey, "he looks like a dreamy Christmas elf," and has an infectious sense of humor, and a voice so soulful it should come with its own harp and halo.

But his fans stay for something else, something more eternal.

His youngest fans might not have the language to articulate it yet; still, it is precisely that search for what's real that turns them into Beliebers and might—only God knows—make more than a few of them into humble believers.

TALKING THE TALK

Justin is not shy about mentioning his faith publicly in dozens of interviews, on the red carpet, on Twitter and Facebook, in his film *Never Say Never,* and in his 2010 autobiography, *First Step 2 Forever.* Whether he is prompted by a reporter's question or raises the issue himself, Justin regularly speaks about his personal faith in Jesus Christ and how he believes God's hand guides him through his life. Never defensive—or worse, offensive—in his remarks about eternal things, the thoughts he expresses with great ease are laced with themes of gratitude, humility, faith, and a worldview that is obviously anchored by a generous love.

Here is a selection of some of Justin's statements about his faith:

In a video interview with the Associated Press in Los Angeles, November 1, 2010: "I'm a Christian. I believe in God. I believe that Jesus died on the cross for my sins. I believe that . . . I have a relationship with him and I'm able to talk to him. And really, he's the reason I'm here. So I have to definitely have to remember that. As soon as I start forgetting, you know, I have to like, click back and be like, ya know, this is why I'm here."

At a London press conference in May 2011 before the UK premiere of *Never Say Never:* "Who is my biggest role model? Um . . . does it have to be, like, in this day and age?" (Anybody at all.) "At all? OK . . . Job. I'm serious. Do you guys wanna know why? Do you guys know who Job is? Yes, from the Bible. OK, so, he got tortured, like, he got his family killed. Everything was taken away from him—his job, his cattle. And yet he still remained, like, still faithful to God and still trusted God after everything was taken away. And he was, like, he didn't know why it happened, but he still put his faith in God and remembered that, like, everything happens for a reason. So that's why."

From his autobiography, *First Step 2 Forever: My Story* (page 84): "On stage, we don't want any surprises. We want everything to play out perfect, just the way we planned. In life, you get the full reveal. It's all a surprise. And that makes it a lot more interesting, even though some of the surprises suck. In the Bible, it says 'everything works together for good' if you love God, but there are times when it does not feel that way at all. Times when you're like, 'Yo, God! This is messed up. Could you pay some attention down here?' Maybe faith is the ability to chill and trust that somebody up there got the set list right. Maybe when you're cool with whatever comes your way, the reveal eventually happens, and even the bad moments can turn around and bless you."

Accepting his award for "Top New Artist" at the 2011 Billboard Music Awards in Las Vegas: "I want to thank God, because ya know, he's blessed me so much. Every day is like crazy to me because I see so many people, and I get to make so many people smile and make people happy. And this is like, it's crazy that I'm surrounded by so many amazing people, and I just, I don't know. I want to thank my fans again for being so amazing. And my mom. Mom, you've been amazing. You've been traveling with me, putting up with all my crap. I love you . . . I want to thank my whole team because my team together they help me to stay young and stay normal, kind of."

On the Red Carpet at the 2011 Oscars (via WLSQ.tv): "I think it's really great that I have God in my life. He's probably the number one reason I'm here. Without God, I don't know what I'd do. He keeps me humble."

On *The Ellen DeGeneres Show* (Feb. 2011): "I think it's cool because there are so many talented people. And that's like, God has blessed so many people. And it takes a lot of hard work as well. He wants you to really work for it and he wants you to always just trust him."

On *Live! with Regis and Kelly* (Feb. 2011): "I've definitely been blessed by God, and he's definitely been very generous to me. And it's just been an amazing roller-coaster ride this . . . last two years."

In May 2011 live interview on New Zealand television (not long after the country was hit by a devastating earthquake), when asked whether he had a message for his fans there: "I'm praying for you guys, with all the devastation you guys are going through. But everything's gonna be all right, and I love you so much."

From *First Step 2 Forever: My Story* (page 175): "I like . . . when people ask about my religion (because I love God and I don't want to miss an opportunity to share that)."

During a TV interview backstage at the 2010 American Music Awards: "I think that God is really the only one keeping me sane right now."

Backstage before a performance in Paris (from the 2010 *E! News Special* "Justin Bieber: My World"): "Lord, thank you for this day and thank you that I get to travel the world."

From *First Step 2 Forever: My Story* on his mother, Pattie Mallette (page 42): "After she had me, she had to work really hard all the time, but she never complained. She let me be myself, but she kept an eagle eye on me, stayed strong about discipline, and impressed on me the importance of doing the right thing and keeping God in my life. I admire her so much for how she learned from her mistakes, got her life together, and made a life for me."

Free-style rapping in 2010 on the New Zealand television program *Select Live*: "My love, yeah, it's overflowing. I gotta show you a place where I go just to think about things. It's the top of the world with the King of Kings."

From the song "Won't Stop" on Sean Kingston's *King of Kingz* **mixtape, from the rap Justin wrote himself:**
Every person in this world can do good.
I just want this message understood.
Alright . . . stop.
Everybody's gotta listen make the decision to envision a better place with no division.
Religion.
Everybody needs a mission. Haters need to stop it, just listen.

Interview with Swiss television in Zurich (April 2011):
"I think everything happens for a reason. I think God picks certain people and he blesses certain people with different talents and different things. And, ya know, I just have to remember what I'm here for and that he put me in this position."

Backstage before a concert with his crew via *60 Minutes Australia* **(April 2011):** "Dear Lord Jesus, thank you so much for this tea. And thank you so much for my dancers. And thank you so much for my backup singers."

From *First Step 2 Forever: My Story* on meeting his manager, Scooter Braun (page 113): "Mom decided this Scooter guy in the purple pimpmobile was okay after all. He had a strong Jewish faith. His family [was] loving, rock solid and successful. Sure he was young, but he was polite and super-motivated. He knew a lot about the business. And he believed in me."

On *60 Minutes Australia* when asked "You have quite firm family values and Christian values as well, don't you?" (April 2011): "Mmm, hmm. I'm a Christian. I believe that Jesus died on the cross for my sins. And uh, it helps me stay grounded, being able to pray and stuff. And to keep that more important than anything else. Because if you start taking yourself more seriously than you do God, then there's a problem."

On Straits TV (April 2011): "I was in Israel and I was in a church and I was looking at different places, ya know, where Jesus walked and stuff. And that was just kinda really important to me. It just kind of sucked that [the paparazzi] didn't have any respect. They were coming in the churches and that kind of aggravated me. They were coming into the churches and stuff. I thought that they'd have a line, but they just crossed it there."

From *First Step 2 Forever: My Story*, describing a huddle backstage at a show in Hartford, Connecticut, on June 22, 2010 (page 236): "My team gathers in a tight huddle. Mom thanks God for all the blessings that have poured out on us. Mama Jan [his vocal coach] prays that my voice will be empowered with love. I pray for the safety of me and my dance crew and everyone above and below the stage. Dan leads us in an ancient Hebrew prayer Scooter taught us. 'Sh-ma Yis'ra'eil Adonai Eloheinu Adonai echad.' (Hear, oh Israel, that the Lord is our God, the Lord is One.)"

From the film *Never Say Never*, while saying grace at a pizza restaurant with friends: "Thank you, Lord. Thank you that we have great friends and we're able to hang out together and have a good time."

On *Entertainment Tonight* (Feb. 2011): "I want to plant in people's lives to just be like, anything is possible. If you put God first, and remember to always stay humble and always be gracious, ya know, anything can happen."

In his 2010 song "Pray": "I pray for all the souls that need a break, Can you give 'em one today?"

Written message at the end of the "Pray" video, quoting Mother Teresa: "God speaks in the silence of the heart. Listening is the beginning of prayer."

From *First Step 2 Forever: My Story* (page 9): "I'm surrounded by super-smart, super-talented, extremely good people who love me and watch out for me every step of the way. They don't let me lose sight of where I came from or where I'm going. And they don't let me get away with any crap. The success I've achieved comes to me from God, through the people who love and support me, and I include my fans in that. Every single one of you lifts me a little bit higher."

TWEETS OF FAITH

Since he sent his first tweet back on May 12, 2009 (asking his fans to "check out" his new single "One Time"), Justin has been giving his millions of fans around the world an inside, real-time peek into his world, his heart and his soul.

In dozens of tweets over two years, Justin has talked about his faith, sent words of encouragement and spiritual inspiration, asked for prayer, and urged his fans to pray for others in need. He's also expressed his gratitude to God (and his fans) for the blessings he's been given and has encouraged his followers to have faith and believe.

Here are all of his "tweets of faith" from May 2009 through June 2011. It's a quite a testimony to one young man's faith and to the grace of a loving God.

@justinbieber	Aug 22 2009, 21:46	Just landed and found out someone I care about got in a bad accident and is fighting for her life. Everyone please pray for her for me.
@justinbieber	Aug 24 2009, 18:24	In the hospital with my friend...thank you all for your prayers and support. Means alot to her and me. This is a private matter but thank u
@justinbieber	Oct 18 2009, 21:06	once again thanks for everyone for keeping my friend in their prayers...it meant alot as u just saw. love u guys
@justinbieber	Dec 20 2009, 5:30	just woke up feeling incredibly blessed. what a year. u r the greatest fans ever. Thanks

@justinbieber	Dec 24 2009, 6:51	This holiday season i hope we can all appreciate eachother and be happy 4 eachother's blessings. help 1 another the way u have all helped me
@justinbieber	Feb 11 2010, 5:21	want to make this clear. I am blessed and grateful everyday for this new life Im getting to live
@justinbieber	Feb 27 2010, 19:35	Just saw on the news about the earthquake in chile and the possible tsunamis. My prayers go out to those people and their families affected
@justinbieber	Mar 3 2010, 3:34	Respect eachother. Will continue to keep praying for the people of Chile and Haiti #RIPAlejandraJonas
@justinbieber	Mar 14 2010, 21:06	some sunday church...then did a little singing with some friends...ran through U SMILE and BABY and THAT SHOULD BE ME. sounded great
@justinbieber	Mar 30 2010, 6:24	life is a blessing and appreciation for our time here with eachother is important #ripaprilbieber
@justinbieber	Apr 10 2010, 16:30	would b amazing if some1 found the GOLDEN TICKETS during a buyout and they and the kid they helped at the hospital got 2 come 2 the BAHAMAS
@justinbieber	Apr 10 2010, 16:27	heard there is a @NYCbuyout today.... sounds fun. they are donating the cds from the buyout to childrens hospitals. that is incredible....
@justinbieber	Apr 10 2010, 16:27	any1 else planning buyouts? feel blessed to have such incredible fans who actually not only care about the music but helping others. Thanks

@justinbieber	Apr 12 2010, 21:06	thanks to everyone for your prayers for a certain friend of mine...she is doing much better and its good to see her smiling. Thanks
@justinbieber	Apr 13 2010, 5:18	great night with great friends. health and happiness goes a long way. blessed 2 have incredible people in my life. got some weirdos too. Lol
@justinbieber	Apr 22 2010, 0:24	make sure you are watching American Idol's IDOL GIVES BACK right now!! Great cause
@justinbieber	Apr 22 2010, 0:26	also just saw Crystal Bowersox's performance. She is incredible and she is right...Thank the lord http://bit.ly/dmX-Wdr
@justinbieber	May 26 2010, 2:52	family time with my mom couldnt come at a better time....i was raised to respect others and not gossip...nor answer gossip with anger
@justinbieber	May 26 2010, 2:55	i know my friends family and fans know the person i am. hearing adults spread lies and rumors is part of the job i guess.
@justinbieber	Jun 15 2010, 23:51	If your truly my fan u will not put down any of my family members or friends, When you smile i smile, and when my friends hurt i hurt. :(
@justinbieber	Jun 16 2010, 1:03	brush off the haterz n realize life is good n it's a blessing. will always support my friends but no more giving mind 2 haterz. hi haterz :0
@justinbieber	Jun 20 2010, 18:00	we r having fun today but make sure 2 tune in 2morrow as we do what we can to help those in need in the Gulf - http://tinyurl.com/2f9s5m3

@justinbieber	Jun 20 2010, 18:03	we are blessed everyday...let's share our blessings with others
@justinbieber	Jun 22 2010, 4:03	Wow long night... Bout to catch some zzzzzzzzz... But first I'm gonna say my prayers :) night ladies
@justinbieber	Jun 28 2010, 21:03	If the Lord can forgive so can I....
@justinbieber	Jul 10 2010, 6:17	goodnight world...went go carting and just had some fun tonight. good to be a kid. enjoy the blessings
@justinbieber	Jul 17 2010, 1:53	@valentina_lovee Sometimes the pressure is a lot but I feel so blessed living my dream and I remind myself to be thankful and appreciative.
@justinbieber	Jul 25 2010, 17:45	RT @Sofiasmile19 @justinbieber i'm going to church in a while, i'm gonna pray for u to follow me = Keep G-d first and stay humble. FOLLOWED!
@justinbieber	Aug 15 2010, 15:24	Im telling u people. Everyday we wake up is another blessing. Go after ur dreams... dont let anyone stop u. NEVER SAY NEVER!! CRAZY SUNDAY
@justinbieber	Sep 11 2010, 20:20	9-11. RIP to all those who lost their lives and god bless those out there remembering their loss
@justinbieber	Sep 24 2010, 14:51	it's a big big world...remember we are blessed and should be grateful for the gifts the lord gives us and the love of our friends and family
@justinbieber	Oct 26 2010, 17:34	just found out about the earthquake in Indonesia. everyone please pray for the people there. #prayforindonesia
@justinbieber	Nov 1 2010, 21:45	just heard the news. my prayers go out to lily allen and her family.

@justinbieber	Nov 2 2010, 18:22	the new song on #MYWORLDSACOUSTIC called "PRAY" is by far @studiomama's favorite song I have ever done. hope u guys will like it 2
@justinbieber	Nov 11 2010, 22:54	my dude @kennyhamilton is a former navy man. Happy Veterans Day Kenny. Here is a preview of #Pray for the soldiers - http://bit.ly/dxlu1r
@justinbieber	Nov 13 2010, 5:39	feeling blessed. gonna surprise some special people tomorrow. VA we here
@justinbieber	Nov 21 2010, 2:49	Can someone tell how to make a change!! I close my eyes, and i can see a better day. I close my eyes and #pray
@justinbieber	Nov 21 2010, 8:36	night world. tomorrow AMA's. Gonna take em to church! #PRAY
@justinbieber	Nov 24 2010, 22:45	I made a promise to you guys when I wrote #PRAY that I would use it to raise money for charity. Im keeping my promise - http://bit.ly/fVKUvo
@justinbieber	Nov 25 2010, 18:25	we all have so much to be #thankful for....Im #thankful for the love of my family friends and of course all of you....
@justinbieber	Nov 25 2010, 18:27	I could write a whole book saying all that Im #thankful 4...but let me just say that every new day is another blessing. #HappyThanksgiving
@justinbieber	Nov 27 2010, 1:16	all jokes aside Im proud of the new album #MYWORLDSACOUSTIC and Im proud of the song #PRAY . we can all make a difference in the world. so..
@justinbieber	Nov 28 2010, 21:45	sometimes i cant be everything everyone wants me to be...but i can try...and i can #pray...and I can #believe....and I can #NEVERSAYNEVER

@justinbieber	Dec 4 2010, 20:37	Just want to let my people in Germany know I won't be on Wetten Dass tonight as an accident has taken place and....
@justinbieber	Dec 4 2010, 20:39	...we all don't think it is right to continue. Please pray for Samuel Koch & his family as we wait and hope for his health and safety.
@justinbieber	Dec 29 2010, 1:55	Chillin and happy. Its been a fun year with a lot of blessings. Some crazy rumors but so much love and memories. We r just gettin started!!
@justinbieber	Dec 30 2010, 23:15	all people are equal and all people deserve respect. but with the respect the lord teaches forgiveness. a new year is coming. let him judge
@justinbieber	Dec 30 2010, 23:17	that's all i really got to say about that. I just wanna make music and do what i love. I wanna give back for my blessings and enjoy 2011...
@justinbieber	Dec 31 2010, 23:01	so my #newyearsresolution is to continue to give back for my blessings and do more than the year before. i wanna #makeachange
@justinbieber	Dec 31 2010, 23:03	so #HappyNewYear and #godbless and let's make 2011 even better. I love all of you and Im still the kid from Stratford and Im never changin!
@justinbieber	Jan 11 2011, 7:22	just heard about the floods in Australia. to all the people out there i send you my prayers. #staystrong
@justinbieber	Feb 2 2011, 2:41	I'm grateful 4 every blessing no matter how small or how big. I promise 2 always stay humble and 2 share my blessings with others. I promise

@justinbieber	Feb 13 2011, 21:29	regardless of what happens today is a GREAT DAY...so blessed and grateful. This is just the beginning. Dream BIG and #NEVERSAYNEVER
@justinbieber	Feb 17 2011, 1:26	@usherraymondiv is a great friend and great mentor...blessed to have him in my life. Kill it in LONDON buddy. I will hold down Paris for u.
@justinbieber	Feb 22 2011, 9:34	just ending the night. my prayers go out tonight to the people of New Zealand. god bless
@justinbieber	Feb 27 2011, 20:01	hope everyone is having a blessed sunday. appreciative 4 this life and thankful 4 the friends, family and fans i get 2 share it with. Thanks
@justinbieber	Mar 11 2011, 17:26	Japan is one of my favorite places on earth...it's an incredible culture with amazing people. My prayers go out to them. We all need to help
@justinbieber	Mar 20 2011, 14:07	I love the people and culture of Japan and I love this fan made video. thank you. #prayforjapan - http://youtu.be/sGl-67zM45U4
@justinbieber	Mar 30 2011, 20:35	for real. Belgium. I never ever thought i would get to be in Belgium. Timmins maybe but not Belgium. lol. #blessed #ilovemyfans
@justinbieber	Apr 7 2011, 17:02	hearing the news in Japan I hope everyone is ok and our prayers go out to you. An incredible place and an incredible people. #prayforjapan
@justinbieber	Apr 9 2011, 15:16	zurich to milan....not complaining. #blessed

@justinbieber	Apr 11 2011, 22:23	im in the holy land and i am grateful for that. I just want to have the same personal experience that others have here.
@justinbieber	Apr 11 2011, 22:29	so im looking forward to this week and i look forward to putting on a great show... thank you for the support. night and God Bless
@justinbieber	Apr 12 2011, 12:16	You would think paparazzi would have some respect in holy places. All I wanted was the chance to walk where jesus did here in isreal.
@justinbieber	Apr 12 2011, 12:18	They should be ashamed of themselves. Take pictures of me eating but not in a place of prayer, ridiculous
@justinbieber	Apr 14 2011, 19:06	NEVER GOING TO FORGET THIS ONE. #BLESSED
@justinbieber	Apr 15 2011, 14:47	last night after the show i was able to see Jerusalem...really incredible experience. thank you for those who helped make it happen....
@justinbieber	Apr 15 2011, 14:48	got to see the wall and the tunnels and even a sacred bath that Jesus could of bathed in. incredible. http://bit.ly/heHc1m
@justinbieber	Apr 15 2011, 14:49	also got to visit Yad Vashem Holocaust Museum. An incredible place and something i will never ever forget.
@justinbieber	Apr 17 2011, 14:02	Israel we started off a little rough...but thank u for a week I will never forget. It's an incredible place. thank u
@justinbieber	Apr 17 2011, 14:03	the fans here have been incredible...the show was amazing...and the place is truly special. My family and I will never forget this week.

@justinbieber	Apr 21 2011, 14:45	time for a shower then team dinner. #southeastasia #blessed
@justinbieber	Apr 27 2011, 14:54	been writing alot of songs on the road. excited to just get this music out later this year and record this summer. #BELIEVE #newmusic
@justinbieber	May 5 2011, 15:17	having a moment. just grateful 2 b here living this life. not gonna waste the opportunity. not gonna be selfish. not gonna get in my own way
@justinbieber	May 17 2011, 22:24	up early in TOKYO...about to be on Meza-mashi TV...walking to set now. #grateful
@justinbieber	May 17 2011, 23:06	finished the show..saw footage of the disaster and seeing kids affected 2day. happy 2 b here. its important. we need 2 b here for eachother
@justinbieber	May 18 2011, 9:56	just met some incredible kids who have been thru alot because of the devastation here in Japan. blessed to meet them and proud to know them
@justinbieber	May 18 2011, 9:57	when you meet kids like that..with all their strength and courage to move on you realize the important things in life. #supportJapan
@justinbieber	May 19 2011, 13:40	dedicated #PRAY to the people of Japan tonight and the OLLG was one of the students i met yesterday. Really special night and a great show.
@justinbieber	May 19 2011, 13:41	great way to end the tour...glad we ended it here in JAPAN. thanks to every-one...now time for a break and time to make #BELIEVE

@justinbieber	May 19 2011, 13:48	from singing in the streets of Stratford to a WORLD TOUR...sitting here taking it all in. blessed. thank you. NEVER SAY NEVER and #BELIEVE
@justinbieber	May 24 2011, 4:09	just heard about the devastation in Missouri....my heart goes out to everyone there and their families. my prayers are with you.
@justinbieber	May 30 2011, 5:44	got my friend @seankingston in my prayers tonight. a true friend and big bro. please keep him in your prayers tonight as well.
@justinbieber	May 30 2011, 18:10	I will continue to pray and support my friend. #getwellsean
@justinbieber	Jun 17 2011, 19:31	hangin with friends. blessed and grateful. nothing wrong with being happy
@justinbieber	Jun 18 2011, 2:47	being known isnt good enough. its what you are known for that matters. think positive live positive. #payitforward
@justinbieber	Jun 24 2011, 23:16	just got off the phone with @seankingston. God is good. glad to see you doing better man. love you bro
@justinbieber	Jun 29 2011, 22:38	been working on new music...this next album is gonna be best so far#BELIEVE
@justinbieber	Jul 23 2011, 11:35	my prayers go out to everyone in Norway and my friend Suniva. #prayfornorway

Chapter 11

Tikkun Olam:
Healing the World

Once you bring life into the world, you must protect it.
We must protect it by changing the world
— ELIE WIESEL, NOBEL LAUREATE AND HOLOCAUST SURVIVOR

In the place where there is no man, strive to be a man.
— FROM THE JEWISH TRACTATE BERACHOT (TALMUD)

Y ou have to become a father figure to this kid."
That is exactly what Scooter's mother told her oldest son
when he announced that Justin Bieber had agreed to be his
client. It's motherly wisdom that Scooter has taken very seriously
and with good reason: he describes his mother, an orthodontist
who recently retired to teach dentistry, as his "conscience."

"My mother said, 'If you do this, it isn't like another kid, like
Asher,'" Scooter recalled. (His first "discovery," Asher Roth, was
in college when the two met.)

Not only did Scooter heed his mother's advice, in characteristic form, he aimed higher, wanting to be the best manager/
friend/backup parent that he could be to his young prodigy. "I
have changed my entire lifestyle for Justin Bieber. I love him like

he's my own blood. I would take a bullet for him, and he knows that. Our relationship goes far beyond music. If he couldn't sing a lick tomorrow, he would still be welcomed in my house every day of his life," Scooter said.

"My mom is the most moral woman I know. She's not a big talker, but when she talks you listen—it's going to be of importance," he said. "I know my compassion for others comes from my mother. Since I was a little boy we spent Christmas at the soup kitchen. I'm Jewish, so my mother would say, 'We're not going to celebrate it, so we might as well help people who need it.'"

Scooter's parents, Drs. Ervin and Susan Braun, raised their children with a very clear sense of morality and ethics drawn from the cornerstone Jewish ideals: education, family, charity, and God. "These are the core values that I was taught to live by and this forms the foundation of my relationship with Justin.

"My parents raised me to follow a higher moral standard. They taught me that every human being is extraordinary. It's up to us to set lofty goals—and then strive to exceed them ... When I was growing up, my father taught me that the true role models aren't athletes and entertainers. Rather [they are] those who do their job to the best of their ability. We have to serve as an example to others. That's the responsibility of any human being, all the more so the responsibility of celebrity. And that's the lesson I'm teaching Justin."

In Judaism, there is a concept called *tikkun olam*, meaning "to repair" or "to heal" the world. Essentially, the concept says every Jew is responsible for the material, social, moral, ethical, and spiritual well-being of the entire world—Jewish and non-Jewish. Everybody is spiritually responsible for the welfare of everybody else. It's like that lyric from U2's song "One": "We're one but we're not the same, we get to carry each other." Some Jews believe that *tikkun olam* is a *mitzvah* or commandment that they, God's "chosen people," are obliged to obey. The Bible describes the Jewish people as "a kingdom of priests and a holy nation" and "a light for the nations," called by God to set an example for the rest of humanity. Christianity, which has its roots in Judaism, teaches the same thing—that faithful believers are supposed to be the "light" and "salt" of the world. "You're here to be salt-seasoning that brings out the God-flavors of this earth," Jesus says in the Gospel of St. Matthew. "If you lose your saltiness, how will people taste godliness? You've lost your usefulness and will end up in the garbage. Here's another way to put it: You're here to be light, bringing out the God-colors in the world."

> "[Justin's faith] doesn't make me uncomfortable or anything.
> I'll just listen, like, if it is true. . . . Since I don't have a religion, I'll
> listen to other people's stories and stuff."
> — Greta, 13, Philadelphia, PA

Together, we all are charged with helping to repair and heal the world, God's world.

When you think about it, there's an almost poetic quality to the story of how God brought Justin and Scooter together. By chance—if you believe in such a thing—a Jewish guy in Atlanta (who has two brothers from Africa) discovers this born-again Christian kid in Canada by following YouTube links that his African-American friend Akon, who is a Muslim, sent him. God has a plan for all of us—every single one of us—and will use any means available to draw our attention to whatever it is. We are all connected. We depend on each other. And the story of one of us is truly the story of all of us. There are many lessons we can learn from people whose faith traditions are different than our own. When I was a freshman in college, a philosophy professor of mine said something that I still think about every day of my life. "All truth," he said, "is God's truth." In other words, if something is true, it comes from God. And it doesn't matter who is saying it or where it comes from. If it's true, at the end of the day, it's from God.

Some Christians may find it peculiar that Justin's Christian faith could be informed by or even enlivened by the faith of his Jewish friends. Well, first of all, Jesus was a Jew. It would behoove Christians to know a whole lot more about Judaism than most of us do. Understanding Judaism and its teachings helps us better comprehend the cultural and historical milieu in which Jesus spent his life on Earth. In my own life, I have been blessed with two rabbis who are among my dearest friends. Through Rabbi Irwin and Rabbi Allen, I have learned more about my own faith than I ever could have imagined. The way they approach the world—that we're not just passing through looking for the fastest escape route, but rather we are put here by God to help make the world better in whatever way we can—often leaves me both convicted by my own inaction (and therefore, lack of faith) and inspired to do more, be more generous, kind, and ever more faithful to the command Jesus gave us to be his hands, feet, and voice in the world. The rabbis' faith has made such an indelible impression on my own (and that of my family) that when my son, Vasco, was baptized as a Christian believer in the Pacific Ocean in October 2010, to mark the occasion his father and I gave him a Hebrew middle name—David, which means "beloved"—and asked his chosen auntie, Lisa, who is Jewish, to be one of his three godparents. We were also deeply honored to have his adopted Jewish grandparents, Rabbi Allen and his wife, Ina, pray a Hebrew blessing over Vasco as he began his new journey of faith, following in Jesus' footsteps.

Justin's friendship with Scooter, his musical director Dan Kanter, and the other Jewish folks who are members of his chosen family obviously has made a similar impression on his young life and faith. The *tikkun olam* ideal that Justin learned from Scooter was clearly imparted to Scooter and his siblings by their parents, who likely learned it from their own parents. Dr. Ervin Braun is a Hungarian immigrant. His parents, who met after the end of World War II, were both Holocaust survivors. His mother spent her teen years imprisoned at Auschwitz, a Nazi concentration camp, and was the sole survivor of her family. His father (who is now deceased) survived both the Dachau and Mauthausen concentration camps. In 1956, when a revolution broke out in Hungary, Ervin's parents took him and fled in the middle of the night in a horse-drawn cart through the countryside, crossing the border into Austria only a few steps ahead of the Soviet tanks. They eventually made their way to the United States and settled in the Queens borough of New York City. Ervin's father had been a dentist but could not practice in the United States, so he took odd jobs, while Ervin's mother worked for a time in a sweatshop. Like so many immigrant families, Ervin's parents wanted their son to have a better life in America's promised land. Hard work and education, they believed (rightly) was the key to making their dreams for their son a reality. So Ervin worked diligently to earn enough money to put himself through college and graduate school, and had his degree in dentistry by his early twenties.

Ervin Braun has compared his family's story to the 1986 Oscar-nominated animated film *An American Tail*, about a Russian-Jewish mouse named Fievel who gets separated from his family while immigrating to the United States (where he believes there are no cats).

"There was no persecution in America—that's what we came here for," Ervin Braun said. "And my own son is a shining example of what opportunities one can find here." As a kid, his family occasionally would drive through neighboring Connecticut. "I thought, *One day I'm going to live in Connecticut.* Swear to God. I always thought there'd be great baseball fields and places for families in Connecticut." Years later, while he was interning at the renowned New York hospital Sloane-Kettering, Ervin saw an ad in a trade magazine for a practice in Connecticut and, with his new bride, Susan, settled in Greenwich, one of the wealthiest communities in the nation, just over the border from New York, about a thirty-minute train ride from Manhattan.

> "I don't think he's trying to push it, like, 'You have to believe in THIS God.' "
> — Greta, 13, Philadelphia, PA

The Brauns' children were raised in one of the most privileged communities in the United States, surrounded by extreme wealth and endless opportunities. But they were brought up to see that life for what it is—a profound blessing that comes with real responsibility to care for and share their good fortune. "My heroes as a kid, I would say, were my father and grandfathers," Scooter said. "I fought with my dad at times, but I wanted to be like him. If I'm half the man he is, I'll be okay." It's not surprising, then, that on Pattie and Justin's first visit to Atlanta back in 2007, when Pattie was wrestling with whether she should trust this twenty-five-year-old who wanted to manage her son's career, Scooter offered to introduce her to his dad, who was passing through town. After visiting with Ervin at an airport restaurant (an extreme sports enthusiast, Dr. Braun had a layover in Atlanta on his way home from a kite-boarding excursion),

Pattie felt confident that Scooter was a man of faith from a solid, loving family who was polite, savvy, and believed in her son. She gave Scooter the thumbs up and hasn't looked back.

Scooter is the eldest of the Brauns' children. He has a younger brother, Adam, a philanthropist, and a sister, Liza, who is a medical student in Tel Aviv, Israel. About a decade ago, the Brauns, who seemingly always had various guests staying at their home—a family of Jewish immigrants from Russia and others in need—learned that two teenage boys from Mozambique, Africa, needed a place to stay for a few weeks. Sam and Cornelio moved into the Brauns' Greenwich home, with its pool, tennis court, and backyard basketball gymnasium. It wasn't long before they became permanent members of the Braun clan.

"I think my adopted brothers Sam and Cornelio gave me a lot of perspective," Scooter said. "When they were thirteen and fifteen, my parents became their legal guardians so they could study in the United States. I was the best man at Sam's wedding—they're my brothers. Sam got married to a girl he met at Brown [University]. Cornelio—we call him 'Big C'—went to American University."

"People always say, 'You guys are great for taking these two kids into your home.' The way my family looks at it is, 'Thank God they came into our home, because they gave us so much perspective, and they added such a beautiful layer to our family,'" he said.

When Scooter talks about Justin, I can hear how much he loves him, how proud of him he is, and what an honor—a blessing from God—Justin is to him and the Braun family. "Justin is one of the best things that has ever happened to me," Scooter said. "I am a better man because of the man I have to be for Justin."

Family—and Scooter clearly considers Justin and Pattie to be members of his—is the number one priority and focus of the life of this young business mogul who recently celebrated his thirtieth birthday. He even has a tattoo on his wrist that says "family" to remind him of what's most important. "I recently had Thanksgiving with my family," Scooter said in February 2011. "My father asked us to go around the table, my cousins and everybody, and say what we hoped to be thankful for the next year. I basically told everyone that the extraordinary life that I have been living for the last year, and the things that I am getting to experience are really once in a lifetime, [and] that if you don't have that family to come home to on Thanksgiving, it's really not worth anything."

Over the four years that they've known one another, Scooter has become a guiding force in Justin's life. (Several media outlets have even called Scooter some variation of "Justin's surrogate Jewish father.") It's a role Scooter has embraced with absolute seriousness. No one wants to see Justin wind up like so many other child stars whose lives have careened out of control into a morass of drugs, destruction, and narcissistic excesses that are the stuff of parents' nightmares.

"I'm not going to let that happen to him," Scooter says. "My father would tell me that if no one in the room is being a man, you must stand up and be a man . . . With Justin, I find myself sounding like my father a lot. . . . The only way I'm going to have Justin transcend into an adult artist and continue the career he wants is if he understands the responsibilities he has. If I don't teach him how to be a man, he's not going to be able to handle any of the pressure, or to take any accountability for his own actions, and he's going to grow up to be exactly what everybody is expecting him to be, which is the teen star who then gets into drugs and alcohol and blows it all away.

"I tell him, 'Let me make this clear to you, Justin. You are not normal, you are extraordinary; so you will be held to extraordinary standards, which is the way I was raised', " he said.

Scooter, in partnership with Pattie, has carefully chosen members of the team of people who work the closest with and spend the most time with Justin—his "road family." There is his bodyguard, Kenny Hamilton; his "swag coach," Ryan Good; tour manager, Alison Kaye; vocal coach, Jan "Mama Jan" Smith; and musical director, Dan Kanter. His closest advisors and everyone who works with Team Bieber are governed by one unbreakable rule: don't indulge the teen pop star.

"If you treat him like a superstar, you're fired immediately," Scooter said. "We don't coddle him. We hold him up to being responsible. We demand that he shows respect to people. If he makes a mistake, he has to apologize. Our job is not only to guide his career, but to make sure he grows up to be a good man."

Scooter's management of Justin's life ranges from the big picture—brokering multimillion-dollar business deals, artistic direction, making sure every project the singer is involved with includes a significant charitable component built in, overseeing the production of his documentary film and world tour—to the down-and-dirty hands-on work of raising a teenager on the cusp of manhood. Scooter is not above chasing Justin down and sending him back to his room when he catches the singer riding his skateboard through the halls of a hotel while he's supposed to be resting before a show. He's Pattie's backup in disciplining Justin on the rare occasion when his mother isn't there to do so herself, and has been known to confiscate Justin's cell phone and laptop or cancel an event as a punishment for misbehavior.

Justin has a curfew, which the team enforces religiously, and a modest spending limit on the one credit card he's allowed to carry. It's all a part of Team Bieber's concerted effort to keep Justin as normal, healthy, and well-adjusted as possible under the extraordinary circumstances of superstardom and the nonstop glare of the international media spotlight.

Despite their religious differences, Scooter makes sure Justin remains spiritually healthy as well. He encourages Justin, who rarely gets a chance to attend church services because of his insanely busy touring schedule, to do a Bible study on Sundays. "I think it's good for him to think there's something bigger than himself," Scooter says.

In April 2011, when Justin's world tour was scheduled to make a stop in Tel Aviv, Israel, downtime was built into the performer's schedule so that he could explore the Holy Land for the first time with his family. Both of Justin's parents joined him in Israel, a pilgrimage that held enormous spiritual significance for the young Christian who tweeted about how much he was looking forward to "walking in the places where Jesus walked."

The whole Braun clan joined the Holy Land pilgrimage, including Scooter's Hungarian grandmother. Justin introduced Scooter's *bubbe* on stage during his encore, explaining to the cheering crowd that she is a Holocaust survivor—before singing his most explicitly spiritual song, "Pray." Justin's concert at Tel Aviv's Yarkon Park took place a few days before the beginning of Passover, the Jewish holiday that commemorates God's delivering the Israelites from slavery in Egypt, as told in the biblical book of Exodus. It is one of the most widely celebrated of the Jewish festivals, lasting seven or eight days, and is a time when Jewish families around the world gather for *Seders*, ritual feasts that mark the start of Passover where, traditionally, multiple generations of a family share a meal and read aloud the story of the Israelites' exodus from Egypt. While in Tel Aviv, Justin asked Scooter to adjust the tour schedule so he could experience a *Seder* in Israel.

> "[Justin's faith] only makes me like him more because I am of that religion too. But even if he was a different religion, I wouldn't see anything wrong with it. I wouldn't like him any less."
> — Hannah, 12, St. Louis, MO

Despite that drama involving overzealous Israeli paparazzi, Dan Kanter, who met his wife, Yael, in Israel in 2003 on a Birthright Israel pilgrimage for Jewish youth, said that in the end Justin's Holy Land experience was "amazing" and "very emotional," and confirmed that the young pop star was able to see all that he'd hoped to see (and indeed walk where Jesus walked).

Kanter, who opened the show in Tel Aviv with a Jimi Hendrix-style rendition of the Israeli national anthem, the "Hatikvah," that brought the 40,000 fans to their feet, cheering at near ear-splitting volume, said Justin's appearance in Israel was powerfully meaningful to his young Israeli fans. "They have been a really strong presence and they have been writing and begging him to come to Israel for a couple of years now," he said. "So many other acts have canceled concerts there [because of security and political concerns amidst the ongoing turmoil in the region], so for Justin to go and put on a show—there was a vibe in the air that night . . . It was definitely one of the most exciting audiences he has ever played for."

One tale from Bieber legend in particular really resonated with Israeli Beliebers. They all knew the story: "Justin prays the Shema! He says a Christian prayer and then he says the Shema!"

It's long been a tradition for Justin, Pattie, and the whole crew to pray backstage before every concert. Most often Pattie leads the prayers—for God's blessing on the concert, for the safety of Justin and his backup dancers and singers, for the fans to be blessed by Justin and his message—and she would end her prayer, as is the custom for many born-again Christians, "in Jesus' name." Scooter and Dan are always present for the prayers and grew increasingly uncomfortable with the exclusively Christian themes of the pre-concert "prayer circles." So they decided to add their own prayer called the "Shema"—the most important prayer in the Jewish tradition—at the end. "I felt like if we were going to say a prayer 'in Jesus' name, amen' that Dan and I should be represented as well," Scooter said. "We'd do the same if we had some Muslim or Hindu in the group—we're all-inclusive."

A few concerts into the 2010 tour, they started to recite the Shema—*Sh-ma Yis'ra'eil Adonai Eloheinu Adonai echad* (Hear, oh Israel, that the Lord is our God, the Lord is One)—and they noticed that Justin had chimed in too—in perfect Hebrew.

"I asked him, 'What the heck was that?' and he goes, 'I memorized it,'" Scooter recalled. "He was like, 'This is something Jesus would have said, right?' And I said, 'Yes,' and he's like, 'Then I want to say it with you guys.' I explained that it's one of our holiest prayers, and that it means 'the Lord is one,' and he thought that was cool. He knows it's in ancient Hebrew; he knows that Jesus would have said it, and since Dan and I are very close to him, he wanted us to feel included as well. He's a very special kid."

Praying the Shema during their pre-show prayer circle has since become a permanent fixture for Team Bieber (it was even included in Justin's film, *Never Say Never*). In fact, one American rabbi, Jason Miller, figures that, given the number of concerts that he performs, Justin has probably recited the Shema—"the most important statement of Jewish belief"—many more times than the average sixteen-year-old Jewish kid.

"Justin has twenty thousand people a night telling him that he's the greatest thing on earth," Scooter said. "That's why it's so crucial to acknowledge the One above us. Without that awareness, there's no chance of staying grounded."

By all accounts, Scooter has been very successful not only in keeping Justin grounded, but in calling his attention much higher—to the One that they both work for and to their job together, to help heal the world. One song at a time.

Chapter 12

Pay It
Forward

There's nothing worse than a rock star with a cause . . .
But celebrity is currency and we want to spend it this way.

— BONO

What can I give back to God for the blessings he's poured
out on me? I'll lift high the cup of salvation—a toast to
God! I'll pray in the name of God; I'll complete what I
promised God I'd do, and I'll do it together with his people.

— PSALM 116:12

A half-dozen years ago, while backpacking around the world during his junior year at Rhode Island's Brown University, Scooter's younger brother, Adam Braun, had a chance encounter that changed his life—and eventually the lives of scores of children in the developing world—forever.

While traveling through India, Adam met a young boy begging for money on the street. As was his custom when approached by "street kids" in many of the desperately poor regions of the world his round-the-world journey led him to, Adam asked the boy what he wanted more than anything else.

He had asked the question many times before and figured the young Indian's answer would be similar to what he'd heard in the past. A cell phone or an X-Box, perhaps? Or maybe a sports car or a mansion or a million dollars?

The boy's surprising answer was what Oprah Winfrey might call an "Aha!" moment for Adam.

"A pencil."

Adam reached into his backpack, handed the child a pencil, and "watched as a wave of possibility washed over him," he recalled. "I saw the power and promise brought through something as small as giving a pencil to just one child."

> "He has something none of us has. And that's really cool. It's a blessing from God, and I'm praying that he uses it for something good."
> — Carl, 20, Chicago, IL

For the next five years, as he finished his studies at Brown, graduated in 2006, and launched a lucrative career at a top New York City consulting firm, Adam continued to "backpack relentlessly" across the globe, visiting fifty countries on six continents, handing out pencils and pens to children wherever he went.

"I'd come home, I'd work, finish up my classes, and then I would just book an open-ended ticket to a really poor part of the world," he said.

In a remote Guatemalan village, Adam met a father who asked him to read his Bible in English into a tape recorder. "He wanted to listen to my English so he could teach his children," Adam recalled. That encounter struck a chord deep in Adam's heart, reminding him of his own grandparents—Jewish refugees from Europe who came to America after surviving the Holocaust. "My grandfathers emigrated to this country so my mother and father could have a better education," he said. "Both my parents worked really, really hard so my siblings and I could have a better education."

Back in the States, Adam decided he needed to find a substantial way to give back, following his parents' example of "paying it forward" in the world by helping others in need. "The biggest single way I could find to give back was to start Pencils of Promise, build a lot of schools, and inspire kids globally," he said.

In October 2008, just before his twenty-fifth birthday, Adam opened a bank account in his hometown of Greenwich, Connecticut, with a $25 deposit, created a Facebook page, and began hosting fundraising parties for his new charity. The following year, he took a nine-month leave of absence from his consulting job to open Pencils of Promise's first school in Pha Theung, Laos, and shortly thereafter, quit his job at the consulting firm so he could focus entirely on PoP.

About the same time Adam was launching the PoP charity, his older brother, Scooter, was launching the career of his latest musical discovery, fourteen-year-old Justin Bieber. In fact, Justin was one of PoP's earliest supporters, Adam says, long before the teen singing sensation was, well, a sensation. When Adam was contemplating leaving corporate America for his heart's work among the poorest of the poor three years ago, Justin told him it was the right thing to do.

An estimated seventy-five million children worldwide have no access to education. And 98 percent of all illiterate people live in the developing world. Access to education doesn't just make people smarter, it makes them healthier and their communities more stable and prosperous. For instance, in the developing world, a child born to a mother who has had even the most basic education—in other words, she can read and write and has some basic math skills—is 40 percent more likely to live past the age of five. Making education accessible to the poorest among us will make the world a healthier, more just, and more peaceful place for all of us.

As of July 1, 2011, Pencils of Promise had built forty schools for children in Laos, Nicaragua, and Guatemala and was well on its way to reaching Adam's goal of building one hundred new schools by 2012.

Justin is one of PoP's biggest supporters. In mid-April 2011, he helped launch a special fundraising campaign (that he and Adam dreamed up during a vacation together in Africa) with a single tweet:

@justinbieber	Apr 15 2011, 19:56	shoutout to @pencilsofpromise and the new #schools4all campaign helping #makeachange

The Schools4All campaign challenged people—friends, families, community groups, classmates—to get together to raise money for Pencils of Promise with the biggest fundraiser winning a visit from Adam and Justin to their school. Justin and Adam shot a video together and Justin continued to tweet about the campaign—more than two dozen times—to rally the troops in the Bieber Nation.

By the time the contest ended on July 1, 2011, it had raised more than $285,000—enough to build fourteen more schools for Pencils of Promise and help provide education to thousands more children in the developing world.

"Justin is one of the most talented and special people I've ever met in my life," Adam said. "What a lot of people don't realize is he's not a part of Pencils of Promise because he's a celebrity. He's part of Pencils of Promise because he believes in creating good."

In addition to his online support for Pencils of Promise and its Schools4All campaign, Justin also donates $1 from every concert ticket he sells to the charity. (That means for his two sold-out shows at Dublin's O2 Arena in the spring of 2011—28,000 seats each night—Justin donated $56,000 to Pencils of Promise. And those were just two concerts out of more than a hundred he played in 2010 and 2011.)

"I just think that, for me, it just goes past, you know, money," Justin said. "That can help out so much. It's just $1 out of every ticket sold and it can go so, so far."

• • •

Beliebers who follow Justin on Twitter will be familiar with the tags #payitforward and #makeachange.

From the time he joined Twitter in early 2009 through July 1, 2011, Justin posted more than eighty tweets with those tags and a few hundred more tweets about gratitude, making a difference in the world, giving back to others for the blessings God has given him—and encouraging his fans to do the same.

"It's really easy to do something good, whether it's helping an old lady across the street or, you know, just doing something small for your city, helping out picking up garbage—whatever you can do. Little things make such a difference," Justin said around the time he was named among the twelve "most charitable" celebrities of 2010 by DoSomething.org, an advocacy group that encourages charity and volunteerism among American young people. "I have such a big platform, it would be silly if I didn't do something good with it."

Optimism and commitment to *doing* something (and not just hoping) to make the world a better place are qualities that set Justin apart from many of his colleagues in the music industry. When you listen to Justin's song "Pray," he talks about seeing the world with open eyes—with all of its suffering, disease, wars, and injustice—and feeling powerless to do something to help. Rather than wallow in despair, however, Justin tells his fans, there *is* something they can to. They can always pray. Justin's "Pray" stands in sharp contrast to, for instance, John Mayer's hit single "Waiting on the World to Change," where the 33-year-old singer/songwriter bemoans his generation's lack of influence or power to make a change: "It's not that we don't care / We just know that the fight ain't fair."

> "The way he lives life is really inspiring because he takes his fame and everything and turns it into good. Like for the song 'Pray'—in his music video he goes to Africa and talks about how he can pray for people who have less than him. At the Nashville concert he donated a portion of his proceeds to flood victims, which was really helpful to be a positive influence on other people." — Camille, 14, Nashville, TN

Rather than hopelessness and helplessness, Justin reminds his audience that they do have the power to change the world, whether it's by lifting a prayer, offering a helping hand, raising awareness, or even donating a few dollars. Since his earliest days in the global spotlight as an up-and-coming pop artist, charity has been a hallmark of Justin's career as well as how he sees his mission in the world. One of his earliest tweets, from October 2009, would seem to indicate he was already thinking about how to pay it forward for the amazing blessings and success he'd just begun to enjoy when he asked his Twitter followers, "If you could give to any charity, what would it be?"

Growing up, Justin said, "I didn't have a lot of money—and for me, it's about helping people out who haven't had opportunity." Charities that involve children are particularly close to his heart because he's both inspired by children and is just at the tail end of his own childhood.

"I just love kids . . . In Romania, there are a lot of orphans. There are lots of babies. They're never touched," Justin said, referring to thousands of children in that eastern European nation who spend their childhood institutionalized in crowded orphanages. "They're never, you know, loved and they're never really held, and that's really sad to me. And, for me, I want to go over there and just hold them."

A portion of the proceeds from his album *My Worlds Acoustic* went to the Children's Miracle Network, which raises funds for children's hospitals. "I am in the position to give back thanks to my fans and God," he said at the time of the album's release. "I wrote 'Pray' thinking I wanted to help others and I feel like I have a responsibility to do so. What is the point of doing all this if you can't make a difference in others' lives? This album is a gift to my fans and the money raised from it allows us all to help out."

Justin makes a point of trying to visit patients in children's hospitals wherever he travels on tour, and regularly meets personally with a child from the Make-A-Wish foundation at his concerts. An encounter with one young girl from Make-A-Wish in particular moved him deeply.

"They flew from Australia to come over here," he recalled. "She came and she was so excited and all she wanted was a kiss. I gave her a kiss on the cheek. It makes you realize how much you have when you see people like that." What does he get out of those encounters? "For me, I just like making people smile."

Well, mission accomplished! Justin certainly makes millions of fans around the world smile, but he does more than that. Still in his teens and just a couple of years into his public career,

Justin is fast becoming a standard-bearer for how celebrities can use their influence wisely. The list of charitable organizations and projects that Justin has been involved with since 2009 is vast. His efforts range from the large-scale—such as his work with Pencils of Promise and the Children's Miracle Network—to one-time events and simple, individual acts of kindness.

For example, in spring 2010, Scooter helped Justin launch a contest for schools to support the Women and Children's Hospital in Buffalo, New York. The school that collected the most pennies would win a free concert by Justin himself. The contest ended up raising $152,000—15.2 million pennies weighing more than forty tons!

In February 2011, he had his famous "swoosh" cut into a shorter, spiky do—much to the dismay of millions of Beliebers who expressed their outrage on Twitter for weeks. Afterward— at the request of talk-show host Ellen DeGeneres, with whom he's been friendly for several years—Justin agreed to donate the hair clippings to charity. The remnants of his former "swoosh" eventually netted more than $40,000 at an auction, which he then donated to The Gentle Barn, a rescue facility for severely abused animals that is a favorite of DeGeneres.

When Justin turned seventeen a few weeks later, he asked his fans to donate to the organization Charity: Water in lieu of sending him gifts. Through donations made to Charity: Water's website on Justin's behalf, Beliebers raised $45,000 for the organization that works to make clean, safe drinking water available to the estimated 1.8 billion people worldwide who currently lack access to it. The funds raised for Justin's birthday were enough to provide more than 2,300 people with a permanent source of clean drinking water.

In the fall of 2009, six weeks before his first album dropped,

Justin took time out from preparing for his world debut to record a public service announcement for People for the Ethical Treatment of Animals (PETA) urging people to adopt pets from shelters rather than buy them at pet shops. "My dad and I used to go and hang out . . . just go and visit the different animals and stuff. It's really important that people adopt," he said. "I really encourage going out to an animal shelter or a place where you can get a dog that has been abandoned or doesn't have a home."

> "He really shows how he is a Christian through his singing. He really offers up to his fans and gives back. I think that's cool of him. He's a genuine, down-to-earth celebrity."
> — Sarah, 14, Franklin, TN

Justin also contributed his own "It Gets Better" video to the anti-bullying campaign founded in the wake of a spate of suicides by teenagers who had been harassed and bullied because they were gay or thought to be gay. Bullying is something Justin has experienced personally, and he's ever quick to speak out against it. In fact, while on tour in Australia in the spring of 2011, he brought Casey "The Bully Punisher" Heynes out on stage in Melbourne to thank him for standing up for himself. In March 2011, a cell phone video of Heynes body slamming a schoolyard bully who had tormented him for years went viral on YouTube, quickly becoming one of the most-watched videos of all time on the site.

Justin has lent his voice to various musical fundraising campaigns, including singing the opening line of the twenty-fifth anniversary remake of the famed "We Are the World" benefit single in 2010. Originally recorded in 1985 by stars including Justin's musical idol, Michael Jackson (who died not long before the anniversary recording was made), to benefit famine relief in Ethiopia, proceeds from the "We Are the World 25" single went toward earthquake relief in Haiti. A year later, when massive earthquakes devastated Japan, Justin donated the acoustic version of his song "Pray" to the *Songs for Japan* benefit album (alongside artists that included U2, Lady Gaga, Justin Timberlake, and Bruce Springsteen). The album raised more than $5 million for Japanese disaster relief. And when Justin performed in Japan in April 2011, he donated the proceeds from his concert in Tokyo to the relief effort.

Scooter has famously said that every business arrangement Justin is involved with must have a charitable component built in "or else we don't do the deal." So all of those Justin Bieber singing dolls, scented dog tags, musical toothbrushes, purple headphones, and OPI nail varnishes benefit charitable causes. When Justin launched his Someday fragrance for women in June 2011, he also announced that every penny of the net proceeds would be given away—to Pencils of Promise and the Make-A-Wish Foundation. A month after its release on June 23, 2011, Justin's fragrance, Someday, had generated more than $30 million in retail sales and was poised to be the bestselling perfume of the year (and the most successful celebrity fragrance launch in history.)

"This isn't just for me," Justin said. "I want to be, you know, a role model, as well as someone that can make a difference."

Brad Haugen, the marketing director for Pencils of Promise, which "wants to be this coming generation's nonprofit," said that's exactly what Justin is doing.

"My feeling is that kids are looking for something to believe in," Haugen said. "We're trying to give that to them, and Justin is a way to open the door."

@justinbieber	Sep 29 2009, 22:30	Check out the cool contest I am running with my friends at PETA http://bit.ly/969lX
@justinbieber	Oct 3 2009, 22:08	if you could give to any charity what would it be?
@justinbieber	Oct 5 2009, 19:16	performed ONE TIME at We Day in Toronto 2day...great cause helping out kids around the world. everyone should get involved. MOD at 5p
@justinbieber	Apr 14 2010, 2:15	just thought about it...the fans in Buffalo raised $200k in pennies for charity...that is 20 Million Pennies!!! WOW!! VERY PROUD!!
@justinbieber	Sep 24 2010, 14:51	it's a big big world...remember we are blessed and should be grateful for the gifts the lord gives us and the love of our friends and family
@justinbieber	Nov 24 2010, 22:45	I made a promise to you guys when I wrote #PRAY that I would use it to raise money for charity. Im keeping my promise - http://bit.ly/fVKUvo
@justinbieber	Dec 31 2010, 23:10	so my #newyearsresolution is to continue to give back for my blessings and do more than the year before. I wanna #makeachange
@justinbieber	Feb 21 2011, 23:35	yeah so it's true...i got a lil haircut...i like it...and we are giving all the hair cut to CHARITY to auction. Details coming soon.
@justinbieber	Mar 2 2011, 9:40	great bday. flew in grandma and got my cake. hung out with friends. got surprised. and you all helped #makeachange with @charitywater

Pay It Forward

@justinbieber	Mar 26 2011, 23:18	we can all help. #makeachange #JAPAN - www.itunes.com/songsforjapan
@justinbieber	May 12 2011, 16:23	I think you're wrong. pretty sure President @BarackObama will keep this promise. #payitforward - http://bit.ly/jocrJy
@justinbieber	Jun 7 2011, 14:50	take your blessings and pay them forward. #makeachange
@justinbieber	Jun 18 2011, 2:47	being known isnt good enough. its what you are known for that matters. think positive live positive. #payitforward

MAKE A CHANGE

*There are so many people in this world that go without,
and there are so many people that are starving, and
there are so many people that just need someone to just
help them.*

— JUSTIN TO CNN, DECEMBER 2010

*Then the King will say, "I'm telling the solemn truth:
Whenever you did one of these things to someone over-
looked or ignored, that was me—you did it to me."*

— MATTHEW 25:40

Give back.

Pay it forward.

Be the change you want to see in the world.

Justin is forever encouraging his fans to do whatever they can to help make the world a better place, whether it is through volunteering, donating to charity, or as he urges in his song, "Pray," lifting up those who need healing or a touch of kindness to God in prayer.

Listed on the following pages are a few of Justin's favorite charities (and a couple of the author's as well) and suggestions for how you can get involved—in big and small ways—in making the world a better place.

JUSTIN'S CHARITIES

CHARITY: WATER

charitywater.org
mycharitywater.org

Charity: water is a nonprofit organization based in New York City, with the goal of bringing clean, safe drinking water to people in developing nations. Founded in 2006 by Scott Harrison, a one-time New York City nightclub promoter, it has helped fund nearly 4,000 projects in 19 countries, benefiting almost 1.8 million people worldwide. As of February 2010, the charity had sent more than $10 million to the developing world. When he turned thirty years old, Harrison began to feel unfulfilled with life, however successful he was by the world's standards. He wanted more—to be more, to *do* more. So in 2004, he left the Big Apple behind and became a volunteer in the African nation of Liberia with the organization Mercy Ships—a global charity that operates the largest nongovernmental hospital ship in the world where it provides free health care, including HIV/AIDS prevention and care to terminally ill patients in the developing world, with a particular focus on West Africa. While in Liberia, Harrison studied problems surrounding education, safety, and health and traced them back to a lack of clean water and basic sanitation systems. Harrison began to tap his extensive network of friends and colleagues to get as many people to support his cause as possible and has been tremendously successful. President Obama even mentioned his work with charity: water in his address to the 2011 National Prayer Breakfast in Washington, D.C.

What you can do:

Through the mycharity: water website, you can create a fundraising campaign of your own (like Justin did for his seventeenth birthday, raising more than $45,000—enough to provide more than 2,300 people with clean drinking water!) and collect donations. After eighteen months or so, you and your friends can see the global positioning satellite (GPS) location and pictures of the water projects you helped make possible.

You might also consider getting your school connected with a school in the developing world that needs help. Bring the charity: water project to your campus and help raise awareness about the water crisis facing kids all over the world.

CHILDREN'S MIRACLE NETWORK

Childrensmiraclenetwork.org

Cofounded by the singer/actor Marie Osmond and her family in 1983 as a small, televised fundraiser, today the Children's Miracle Network is one of the leading children's charities in North America. The network has two simple goals: help as many children as possible by raising funds for children's hospitals, and keep those funds in the community where they were raised to help local children. As of 2011, the Children's Miracle Network had raised more than $4.3 billion for children's hospitals in the United States and Canada—most of it through donations of a dollar or two at a time.

One of the hospitals that receives funds from the Children's Miracle Network is the Children's Hospital of Orange County (choc.org), in Orange, California—about an hour south of Los Angeles. In 2011, fifteen-year-old Cody Day, a friend of author Cathleen's family and a lifelong member of the church they attend in Laguna Beach, California, died after a six-year battle with cancer. Cody received wonderful treatment, care, friendship, and support from CHOC throughout his courageous struggle with cancer. When Cody died on May 28, 2011, his parents, Dave and Dallas Day, encouraged their friends and family to make donations to CHOC on Cody's behalf.

What you can do:

Donations of any amount—even a single dollar—can be made online through the Children's Miracle Network website, childrensmiraclenetwork.org. Parents can make a donation by credit card online or by sending a check, and they can even donate their frequent flyer miles or hotel rewards points to help families who must travel far from home so their children can get the medical treatment they need.

Every Children's Miracle Network Hospital has opportunities to volunteer on a local level that you can find on the network's website. They also host a number of fundraisers throughout the year, from dance marathons and radio-a-thons to National Pancake Day at International House of Pancakes (IHOP) and the Dairy Queen Miracle Treat Day. Get involved in whatever way you can and please encourage your friends and family to do the same.

MAKE-A-WISH FOUNDATION

Wish.org

In 1980, seven-year-old Chris Grecius of Phoenix, Arizona, was fighting for his life with terminal leukemia. Chris had always dreamed of someday becoming a police officer. He would ride around his neighborhood on his battery-powered three-wheeled mini-motorcycle writing "tickets" and putting them on car windshields. On April 29, 1980, with the help of a U.S. Customs Officer and a number of other kind-hearted folks in the local police forces and hospital where Chris was being treated, his dream came true. Little Chris got his wish, going on a helicopter tour of Phoenix, visiting police headquarters, "driving" a patrol car (on the lap of an officer), and even being sworn in as an honorary patrolman. On May 1, 1980, police presented him with his own official (specially made in his size) patrolman's uniform. Two days later, Chris died.

That's how the Make-a-Wish Foundation began. In the thirty-plus years since, the foundation has reached more than 250,000 children with life-threatening conditions around the world, making their dreams and wishes come true and has become one of the world's best-known charities. A network of nearly 25,000 volunteers enable the Make-A-Wish Foundation to do their extraordinary work. Today, a wish is granted every forty minutes.

What you can do:

Visit the Make-A-Wish website (wish.org) to make a donation in honor of a loved one, become a monthly giver, volunteer at foundation events, offer your services as a language interpreter or translator, or find out how to organize an event at your school to raise funds for Make-A-Wish. Through its website, you can also learn how to donate your "treasures": supplies, computer equipment, hot tubs and spas, frequent flyer miles, hotel loyalty points, shopping sprees, and more.

You could also adopt a wish. For each child's wish, the Make-A-Wish Foundation covers all expenses associated with the experience for the entire family. The national Adopt-A-Wish program allows individual donors to fund the entire cost of a child's wish. Most wishes fall into one of four categories: *I wish to go . . ., I wish to have . . ., I wish to be . . ., I wish to meet . . .* But a wish can be as creative as a child can imagine. By funding a specific wish, you can create special memories for a child—and for yourself. For more information, please call (800) 722-9474 or email AdoptAWish@wish.org.

JUSTIN'S CHARITIES

PENCILS OF PROMISE

Pencilsofpromise.org

As a junior at Brown University in Rhode Island, Adam Braun (Scooter's younger brother) found himself backpacking through India. There he met a young boy begging on the street and asked the child what he wanted more than anything else in the world. "A pencil," the boy answered. "I reached into my backpack, handed him my pencil, and watched as a wave of possibility washed over him," Braun says. "I saw then the profound power and promise brought through something as small as giving a pencil to just one child." Adam spent the next five years traveling the world, handing out thousands of pens and pencils as a means to start conversations with the people he met on six continents. In 2008, he founded Pencils of Promise with a $25 deposit, hoping to build just a single school. Happily, his project took off, and in three years Pencils of Promise has built forty schools in the developing world—where more than 75 million children live without access to education.

What you can do:

Pencils of Promise has teamed with several apparel and accessories companies to make it easy—and fashionable—to help its cause. Visit www.shoppop-now.com where you can purchase a package of POP stickers for $5, a five-pack of pens for $12, T-shirts, neckties, flip-flops, journals, bracelets, and other items for sale with the profits going to POP's building projects. At the shoppop-now.com site, you can also sponsor a child for a year ($120) or an entire school for a year ($500).

At www.pencilsofpromise.org, you can learn how to organize a fundraiser at your school or house of worship, about volunteer opportunities, and about how you can make donations—and not just money. Follow the links on the POP website to donate your Twitter and Facebook statuses too. Use your voice and your social network to spread the word and help kids in the developing world learn, grow, and meet their unlimited potential and promise.

PEOPLE FOR THE ETHICAL TREATMENT OF ANIMALS (PETAKIDS)

Petakids.com

People for the Ethical Treatment of Animals (PETA) is the largest animal rights organization in the world, with more than two million members. Founded in 1980, PETA believes that all animals deserve the most basic rights—whether they are "cute" or "useful" to us humans or not. Animals can feel pain and are capable of suffering, just like we are. PETA focuses its attention on the four areas in which the largest numbers of animals suffer the most intensely for the longest periods of time—factory farms, laboratories, the fur trade, and the entertainment industry. PETA also works on a variety of other issues including the cruel killing of beavers, birds, and other "pests" and the abuse of backyard dogs. PETA accomplishes its goals through public education, cruelty investigations, research, animal rescues, legislation, special events, celebrity involvement, and direct action.

What you can do:

PETAKids publishes a great magazine called *Kids' Guide to Helping Animals* that has everything you might need to start being a hero for animals. Inside, you'll get tips on everything from protecting wildlife to buying cruelty-free products to organizing animal-friendly field trips. You'll also get the scoop on why so many Hollywood celebs (like Justin!) are helping animals. Visit petakids.com.

IT GETS BETTER

Itgetsbetter.org

It Gets Better is an Internet-based project founded by nationally syndicated columnist Dan Savage on September 21, 2010, in response to the suicide of Billy Lucas, Raymond Chase, Tyler Clementi, Ryan Halligan, Asher Brown, and Seth Walsh and a number of other teenagers who were bullied because they were gay or because their peers suspected that they were homosexuals. The goal of It Gets Better is to prevent suicides among lesbian, gay, bisexual, and transgender youth by having LGBT adults spread the message that their lives will improve. They won't always be bullied, afraid, ashamed, or in despair. It does get better!

The project took off like wildfire with more than 200 videos uploaded in the first week. The project's YouTube channel maxed out its 650 video limit by the second week. The project has since launched its own website, the It Gets Better Project (itgetsbetter.org), which includes more than 10,000 posts and videos from people of all sexual orientations, all over the world.

To date, the project has received submissions from celebrities, organizations, activists, politicians, and media personalities, including President Barack Obama, U.S. Secretary of State Hillary Clinton, Matthew Morrison of *Glee*, Joe Jonas, Joel Madden, Ke$ha, and actors Colin Farrell, Anne Hathaway, and Ellen Degeneres.

Justin recorded his own anti-bullying "It Gets Better" video in November 2010 after appearing on Degeneres' television talk show.

What you can do:

Speak up! If you're being bullied, tell someone—a parent, teacher, adult friend, police officer, principal, pastor, rabbi, imam, older sibling. Don't suffer in silence.

And if you see someone being bullied, well, take a cue from Justin who in his "It Gets Better" video, says: "I just wanted to say there's nothing cool about being a bully. And if you're getting bullied, make sure to tell someone and, you know, it gets better. And if you're a bystander, make sure to step in and, you know, help out."

JUSTIN'S CHARITIES

On March 22, 2011, six months following the launch of the campaign, the It Gets Better Project book was released. *It Gets Better: Coming Out, Overcoming Bullying, and Creating a Life Worth Living* includes essays and new material from more than a hundred contributors, including celebrities, religious leaders, politicians, parents, educators, young people just out of high school, and many more. All proceeds from the book will be donated to LGBT youth charities, including The Trevor Project, which runs a 24/7 toll-free hotline for youth who are considering suicide. If you need help or know someone who does, call the Trevor Project at 866-4-TREVOR (866-488-7386) or visit www. thetrevorproject.org.

CATHLEEN'S CHARITIES

GLOBAL ALLIANCE FOR AFRICA

Globalallianceafrica.org

Back in 2005, when Cathleen was a reporter for the Chicago *Sun-Times* newspaper, one of her colleagues there climbed Mt. Kilimanjaro in Tanzania as a charity fundraiser for Global Alliance for Africa, an organization that works largely with women and children in AIDS-ravaged East Africa through micro-lending, education, and vocational training programs. The following year, Cathleen's colleague was selling raffle tickets for Global Alliance's annual fundraiser. The grand prize was a two-week trip for two people to visit some of the organization's projects in Tanzania, Kenya, and Zanzibar. To her great surprise, Cathleen won!

In the fall of 2007, Cathleen and her husband traveled to Africa. The experience was life changing in many ways. They met dozens of women and children (many of them HIV-positive widows and AIDS orphans) whose lives have taken a turn for the better in innumerable ways through the Global Alliance micro-lending programs. A $75 loan to a single woman can mean she is able to buy school uniforms for her children so they can attend public school, start a weaving or agriculture business, buy better food and health care, and even provide running water or electricity for her family and neighbors in some of the largest slums in the world.

It was on their trip to Africa in 2007 that Cathleen and her husband met the boy who is now their son. Vasco, who turns twelve in October 2011, was an AIDS orphan who had been born with a major heart defect and was dying when they met him by the side of a dusty road in Malawi. He eventually came to the United States for life-saving heart surgery— provided for free by the wonderful doctors at The Heart Institute for Children at Advocate Hope Children's Hospital outside Chicago in June 2009—and in June 2010 became Cathleen's forever son when the High Court of Malawi approved his adoption. He is now a healthy, happy and thriving, soccer-playing, surfing, snow-boarding sixth grader.

One person can make a difference. And a little money can go a long way in the developing world. Cathleen has seen this firsthand.

What you can do:

Through the Global Alliance for Africa's website (www.globalalliance africa.org) you can make a financial donation online to help support their programs, including the micro-lending efforts in Kenya and Tanzania. Even a small donation is helpful. Remember, $75 is a nice dinner out in the United States, but it can mean that a mom in Africa can send her kids to school for the first time and start a business that makes their lives better in innumerable ways.

You might consider joining one of the GAA's treks up Kilimanjaro or sponsoring a climber. Through the website you can even design your own personal fundraising campaign to help support one of the GAA's specific projects—such as their brilliant job-training program in Arusha, Tanzania, for the local guides who take thousands of international travelers up the mountain each year—or provide support more broadly for the Alliance's life-changing work in Africa. And don't forget to buy a raffle ticket. You never know where it might lead!

THE ONE CAMPAIGN & PRODUCT(RED)

ONE.org
Joinred.com
Theglobalfund.org

Cofounded by Bono of U2 and other campaigners, ONE is a grassroots advocacy organization that fights extreme poverty and preventable disease, particularly in Africa, by raising public awareness and pressuring political leaders to support smart and effective policies and programs that are saving lives, helping to put kids in school, and improving the futures of millions of people in the developing world. Backed by a movement of more than 2.5 million members, ONE holds world leaders to account for the commitments they've made to fight extreme poverty, and campaigns for better development policies, more effective aid, and trade reform. ONE also works to support better democracy, accountability, and transparency to ensure policies to beat poverty are able to work effectively. As a result of those programs and policies, today nearly 4 million Africans have access to life-saving AIDS medication, up from only 50,000 people in 2002. Malaria deaths have been cut in half in countries across Africa in less than two years and 42 million more children are now going to school.

What you can do:

ONE is not a grant-making organization and does not accept financial donations from the general public. As Bono always says, at ONE, "We're not asking for your money, we're asking for your voice."

You can join the ONE campaign in less than a minute by visiting its website, www.one.org. There you can read news and blog posts about the latest ONE campaign projects and developments; sign various petitions supporting programs and legislation (in the United States and abroad) that seek to help those struggling with extreme poverty and diseases such as HIV/AIDS, malaria, and tuberculosis (TB) get the help they so desperately need; and fill out an online form to send a letter directly to your senator or congressman/congresswoman encouraging them to support foreign aid bills and other legislation meant to help the least of those among us.

The ONE campaign recently introduced a new app for smartphones (iPhones, Droids, Blackberries, etc.) to help keep ONE members connected with what ONE is doing, including up-to-the-minute messages about how to get involved and what the most pressing issues of the day are. You can download it from the one.org site.

Through ONE's partner brand, (PRODUCT)RED, you can turn a shopping trip to the mall into a charitable act that will help suffering Africans. Founded in 2006 by Bono and Bobby Shriver (the older brother of Maria Shriver and nephew of the late U.S. President John F. Kennedy), (PRODUCT)RED works with companies such as Apple, Nike, The Gap, American Express, Converse, and Starbucks to brand everything from computers and sneakers to cappuccinos and credit cards with the RED logo. When you purchase one of the RED-branded items, a portion of the proceeds goes directly to the United Nation's Global Fund to Fight AIDS, Tuberculosis, and Malaria. By 2011, sales of RED merchandise had provided more than $170 million to the Global Fund, investing 100 percent of its RED dollars into programs that fight HIV/AIDS in Africa, particularly among women and children.

Join RED and find out where you can purchase RED-branded items at www.joinred.com.

Created in 2002, the Global Fund has committed $21.7 billion to fund life-saving programs in 150 countries in the developing world. Today, programs supported by the Global Fund have prevented more than 6.5 million deaths by providing AIDS treatment for three million people,

TB treatment for nearly 8 million people, and by the distribution of 160 million insecticide-treated bed nets for the prevention of malaria worldwide. For more information about the Global Fund, visit www.the-globalfund.org.

RONALD MCDONALD HOUSE CHARITIES

rmhc.org

Many families travel far from home to get treatment for their seriously ill or injured children. Often, it can be a long time to be away from home, or it can divide a family. And for children facing a serious medical crisis, nothing seems scarier than not having their mom and dad close by for love and support. When Vasco was in the hospital undergoing surgery to correct his heart defect, Cathleen and her husband stayed at the beautiful Ronald McDonald House right across the street from Hope Children's Hospital/The Heart Institute for Children in Oak Lawn, Illinois. Vasco could see the McDonald house from his hospital room window, and it was a huge comfort to him (and his folks) to be able to be so close by in those difficult days.

The Ronald McDonald House program provides a "home away from home" for families so they can stay close by their hospitalized child at little or no cost. The McDonald houses are built on the simple idea that nothing else should matter when a family is focused on healing their child—not where they can afford to stay, where they will get their next meal, or where they will lay their head at night to rest. Families are stronger when they are together, which helps in the healing process. Cathleen and her husband only stayed at the Oak Lawn McDonald house for about a week while Vasco recovered from surgery, but while they were there, they met dozens of parents and families who had called the house their home for weeks and months at a time. It's a massive blessing for these families, and it was a huge grace to Vasco and his new parents even for the short time they stayed there.

Every McDonald house has a huge, fully equipped kitchen where families can cook their own meals or help themselves to trays of home-cooked meals provided daily by volunteers from the surrounding community. There are private bedrooms and playrooms for children well-stocked with brand-new toys, as well as laundry facilities, televisions, and libraries full of books, music, and DVD movies. The houses don't feel like hotels or sterile institutions. They are warm, welcoming, and filled with love and hope. They are homes in every sense of the word. The accommodations at McDonald houses cost about $85 per family per night, but families are asked only to make a donation up to $25 per day—and only if they can afford to do so. Many families are able to stay in the McDonald houses at no cost at all because of the generosity of thousands of donors around the world. No family is ever turned away because of money.

What you can do:

There are tons of ways to get involved with supporting the Ronald McDonald Houses. (Visit http://rmhc.org/how-you-can-help) for a long list.) But perhaps the easiest way is to donate money to the homes through their website. According to 2009 figures for the Ronald McDonald Houses:

- Average cost to host a family for one night = $85

- Daily electricity bill for an average House for one day = $125

- Daily gas bill to keep appliances like a kitchen stove working = $60

- 5 flu vaccinations on a Ronald McDonald Care Mobile = $175

- Saving families from eating in the hospital cafeteria = $25

On the rmhc.org website, you can find the location of the McDonald houses near you and a list of their supply needs. The houses provide everything a family might need during their stay, so they are always looking for donations of paper towels, toilet paper, and other household items. You might also consider getting together with your family or friends to make a meal for the McDonald house near you. There is nothing more comforting after a long day at the hospital than coming home to a delicious meal prepared with love and kindness.

Chapter 13

#BELIEVE

*The fundamental fact of existence is that this trust in
God, this faith, is the firm foundation under everything
that makes life worth living. It's our handle on what we
can't see.*

— HEBREWS 11:1

*I meant to tell you there's no limit
To what you can do
You just gotta believe*

— JUSTIN BIEBER, "BELIEVE"

At the time of this writing in late July 2011, it's been about
six weeks since Justin came home from his lengthy "My
World" tour, wrapping things up on May 20 at Tokyo's
Nippon Buddakan. Despite announcing that he was taking a
month off—"to think, pray and just kind of grow up"—Justin
appears to be almost as busy as ever, crisscrossing North America to visit friends, family, and his girlfriend, as well as attending
to a laundry list of professional commitments that makes me
tired just looking at it.

Barely twenty-four hours after he returned to the United States from Japan, Justin was in Las Vegas with his mom, Pattie, and his girlfriend, Selena Gomez, for the 2011 Billboard Music Awards, where he was the biggest winner of the night, picking up six awards in all, including Top New Artist and Top Pop Album for *My World 2.0*. From there he headed to Hawaii for some down time on the beach with Pattie, Selena, and her parents.

Sometime in the past few months, though he hasn't said publicly where and when exactly, Justin got some new ink. In Hawaii, paparazzi snapped Justin shirtless revealing a new tattoo in black ink running a few inches vertically down the left side of his rib cage. The tat was of the Hebrew letters ישוע which spell "YESHUA," the Hebrew name for Jesus. There was great debate online—as there is about seemingly every move Justin makes—about his tattoo and what message he might be trying to communicate through it.

> "I'm curious to see what happens in terms of how he speaks out about his faith once he starts shifting out of the center of the limelight, and if he, like a lot of these other stars, will decide that he needs to start doing these crazy things to stand out."
> — Paul, 20, Dallas, TX

I think it's beautiful. If you're going to get a tattoo (I have a few, all of them words and images connected to my Christian faith), it should mean something deeply personal. The location of the tattoo made me think of the place on Jesus' body where he was stabbed with a sword as he hung on the cross, and I figured it was Justin's way of expressing his commitment to his Christian faith. I wasn't alone in reaching that conclusion. The Rev. Kyle Steven Bonenberger, pastor of City Church in Anaheim,

California, applauded the young superstar's new ink, telling the *Christian Post* he thought it was Justin's way of telling the world he is a person of faith.

The Jesus tattoo was Justin's second (that we know of), joining the small black outline of a seagull he had placed on his left hip when he turned sixteen. Apparently, it's a tradition in the Bieber family for male members to get inked with the bird on their sixteenth birthdays. The outline of a seagull is an homage to the 1970 novella *Jonathan Livingston Seagull: A Story*. It's a fable about a young seagull learning about life, how to fly, and becoming, essentially, the best bird he can be. Justin's father, Jeremy, his uncle, and several other relatives also have the seagull tattoo. Jeremy also got a matching "YESHUA" tattoo at the same time as his son, while a photographer snapped pictures and Adam Braun, Scooter's brother, looked on.

• • •

Fresh off his Hawaiian holiday at the beginning of June, Justin hit the ground running (again), making a surprise appearance at the MTV Movie Awards in Los Angeles (to collect his "Best Jaw-Dropping Moment" award for his performance in *Never Say Never*) before heading to Nashville for the Country Music Television (CMT) Music Awards, where his improbable collaboration with Rascall Flats on his song "That Should Be Me" won the Best Collaborative Video award. Later in the month, Justin attended the MuchMusic Video Awards in Toronto (hosted by Selena), walked the red carpet at the premiere of her new film *Monte Carlo* in New York City, and turned up with his manager, Scooter, for the Black Entertainment Television (BET) Awards in Los Angeles. A few days later, Justin was ringside at an Ultimate

Fighting Championship in Las Vegas with his father, Jeremy, and then flew back across the continent to celebrate the Fourth of July with Selena (and the godfather of hip-hop, Russell Simmons, among others) on a yacht off the coast of Long Island, New York.

The balance in Justin's frequent flier miles account must be humongous because it often seems like he spends more time in the air than he does on the ground.

Somewhere in the middle of his epic travels, Justin found time to launch his ladies fragrance, Someday (the profits from his perfume are going to charity), and promote it on numerous television programs including daytime's *The View* and *Late Night with David Letterman*. On Canada Day (July 1), he received the Bronze Star award from his hometown—an honor akin to getting the "key to the city"—sending his grandparents to accept the honor on his behalf. Rounding out the past weeks came word from the *Guinness Book of World Records* that the video for his song "Baby" officially had become the most-watched video on the entire Internet with 575,118,703 views.

Despite his ridiculously hectic personal and professional schedule, Justin was still up to his old tricks on Twitter, dropping hints about what he's got planned for the near future and causing a frenzy of speculation among the eleven million Beliebers who now follow his tweets. In June and July he dropped what many fans interpreted as a couple of major clues about his next album:

@justinbieber	Jun 20 2011, 19:02	and yes i have been enjoying the time off but when we come back we are coming strong. #BELIEVE that. #november
@justinbieber	Jun 29 2011, 22:38	been working on new music. . .this next album is gonna be best so far #BELIEVE

@justinbieber	Jul 25 2011, 1:58	more excited than ever to get back in the studio and make this #newalbum. miss the tour and want to give u all new music. #BELIEVE

Beliebers interpreted the clues to mean that Justin's new album will be released in November 2011 and be called—maybe? probably?—*Believe*. The title makes sense in the context of Bieber mythology as Justin often encourages his fans to "believe," follow their dreams, and "never say never."

@justinbieber	May 15 2011, 17:56	#BELIEVE and #NeverSayNever
@justinbieber	May 19 2011, 13:41	great way to end the tour. . .glad we ended it here in JAPAN. Thanks to everyone. . .now time for a break and time to make #BELIEVE
@justinbieber	May 19 2011, 13:48	from singing in the streets of Stratford to a WORLD TOUR...sitting here taking it all in. blessed. thank you. NEVER SAY NEVER and #BELIEVE
@justinbieber	May 22 2011, 22:44	almost about that time. . .a little nervous. . .win or lose we are proving to #neversaynever and #BELIEVE

In 2010, Scooter confirmed that Beliebers could expect a new album in 2011 and in the *Rolling Stone* interview in early 2011, Justin mentioned that the title of his next album might be *Believe*. And then in late June 2011, he talked to Perez Hilton.com about working on new material. "I want to work a lot more with myself, and write a lot myself," Justin said. "I will be working with a lot of other producers and stuff like that, but I'm just writing a lot, writing on tour, writing about how I feel and producing. I've been producing on my laptop and on my computer.

"I've been really into it and, hopefully, this next album will be huge. I've done a lot on my acoustic guitar, so it's gonna have that vibe. I'm not gonna really limit myself. I think music is music . . . I mean, I know there's country music, there's rock music, but my music is different. My voice is not meant for any [one] style. I just want to make music."

Dan Kanter also talked about Justin starting to take song-writing into his own hands. "Justin is an amazing songwriter," Dan said. "Backstage, before a show, we'll have some guitars lying around and he'll write songs ... The songs I've heard him writing are much more personal, about what's going on in his life, and I think a lot of his fans will relate to them. That's the secret—for his audience to grow up with him, not grow out of him. I think we'll see issues of traveling, of being away from home, and being in the spotlight in songs on the next album."

Dan said the next album also will likely show how Justin is evolving musically, in terms of its sound. "He loves all styles of music. So who knows if he'll record a heavy metal album one day. But I think it'll continue to be these great, danceable, sing-along songs," he said.

When asked whether fans should expect Justin's music to get "edgier," Dan said, "I'm not sure, but right now I can't see that just because his music is definitely a reflection of his personality—and he's so genuinely happy and nice and easygoing. I don't think there's a reason to be edgy."

> "Justin, I want you to be 17. I don't want you to come up with really prophetic songs ... yet. But I hope that someday, you will come around to that."
> — Carl, 20, Chicago, IL

Justin has worked with artists and producers across the spectrum of popular music from rap, hip-hop, and R&B to country and pop. It's exciting to think about what he might come up with next and with whom. So when I read a post online on April 1, 2011, announcing that Justin would be working with Daniel Lanois, the Canadian artist and producer who has famously worked with U2 on several of their most enduring albums, including my favorite, 1988's *The Joshua Tree*, I believed it. Lanois is also a believer, like Justin and Bono. Visions of Danny shepherding Justin through his own *The Joshua Tree* musical moment danced in my head. I was stoked!

(What I should have been, in hindsight, was a wee bit more attentive to details, such as the date of the "news" item.)

It said:

In a move that has surprised the pop and R&B music world, Daniel Lanois has agreed to produce Justin Bieber's next studio album, despite earlier rumors rapper Kanye West was to help JB's new album project.

Three albums produced by Lanois have won the Grammy Award for Album of the Year, and four others received nominations.

On March 31, manager Scooter Braun spilled, "For some time Justin's been talking about going in a new direction to expand his fan base. After I talked to Daniel Lanois at the Junos, he finally agreed to produce the new album. Justin's ecstatic!"

Scooter Braun mentioned other artists who may be featured in the hitmaker's next effort. "Justin's been talking to Drake about new music," he said. "He's talked with Rascal Flatts. Him and Chris Brown have been sending stuff back and forth to each other. . . . But Lanois is going to be the man in charge."

Daniel Lanois will return to the studio to begin work on the Justin Bieber album in early July 2011. Justin Bieber's own Never Say Never *tour ends May 19 in Tokyo, Japan.*

> "I give up a lot and I quit on things a lot because I get bored. Or I'll say, 'This is too hard; I don't want to do it anymore,' and I'll quit. But Justin kind of inspired me to keep going, and if something's hard, you just have to keep trying."
> — Greta, 13, Philadelphia, PA

I was so excited that I tweeted the story, posted it on Facebook, and even blogged about it. A few days later, I received an email from a friend of mine in Canada who, like me, is a journalist who writes often about the intersection of faith and popular culture. "You did know that post about Lanois and Justin was an April Fool's Day joke, right?"

D'oh! I turned three shades of purple from embarrassment.

Hey, it's a great idea even if it was a joke. So if Scooter, Justin, and Danny are reading this . . .

♥ ♥ ♥

Justin is said to be interested in pursuing a career in acting as well as music—perhaps following the lead of the *other* Justin, Mr. Timberlake, whose baptism into the world of celebrity was as an adorable boy band member when he was still a teenager before crossing over into acting where he has earned some serious chops in critically acclaimed films such as the Oscar-nominated *The Social Network*. Hollywood heavy-hitters Ashton Kutcher, Mark Wahlberg, and even Stephen Spielberg have expressed interest in working with Justin on upcoming film projects, and Scooter has confirmed that Justin and his team are actively reading scripts and that his protégé would "absolutely" be taking acting lessons sometime soon.

As Justin approaches his eighteenth birthday next year, there is also the question of whether he'll continue his formal education. Justin, who travels with a private tutor, says that despite his phenomenal success, he still hopes to attend university. "I want to finish high school and also college," he said, "and then evolve wherever my music takes me."

Only God knows what the future holds for Justin. Will he burn out and fade away? (I wouldn't bet on it.) Or will his starlight grow even brighter, leading him to even more places beyond his wildest dreams?

For this extraordinary young man, I have faith that the best is yet to come.

I still Belieb. I hope you do too.

| @justinbieber | Jul 11 2011, 2:03 | #ilovemyfans, my friends and my family. I give all my blessings to God and appreciate all that i have and will never forget to give back. . . . |
| @justinbieber | Jul 11 2011, 2:04 | . . .there is just too much love to let hate bring you down. thank you for everything and i will always #payitforward and try to #makeachange |

Postscript: A True Story

I treat people as if they were telephones. If I meet some-body who I don't think likes me, I say to myself, "Bob, this one's temporarily out of order." . . . Don't break the connection. Just hang up and try again.

— BOB WILEY IN THE FILM WHAT ABOUT BOB?

The first thing people usually ask me when they hear about *Belieber!: Fame, Faith and the Heart of Justin Bieber* is, "Did you talk to him?"

And the second thing they want to know, when I tell them that I did not, in fact, have an opportunity to interview Justin for the book is, "So, do you think this whole 'Christian' thing is a marketing ploy?" or "Do you think Justin and his team are pulling back from talking about his faith?"

When I set out to write this book, my fear was that if Justin didn't participate in the book directly, some readers would question the authenticity of his faith. So let me state this as plainly as I can: No. He's for real. He's a Christian believer. Of that I'm sure.

In my more than a decade as a journalist, I've had the opportunity to interview and spend time with many celebrities, including heads of state and more than a couple of folks who have ascended to the outer stratosphere of superstardom. The demands on their time and the beyond hectic nature of their schedules is something most of us couldn't even imagine. Everyone wants a piece of them. All the time. They are booked out months, and sometimes years, in advance and adding a new commitment to the mix, even if it's something they really want to do, is sometimes simply impossible.

I did reach out to Justin directly, through his management team, and eventually through family friends and Pattie, his mother. We even built a private website for Pattie so she could see precisely what we were working on, what we hoped to be able to speak to her and Justin about personally, and what we prayed the impact of telling Justin's story of faith in book form would accomplish in the world.

Unfortunately, for whatever reason—see above—I never got a solid answer. They didn't say yes, and they didn't say no. They just didn't respond. I'd be lying if I said I wasn't disappointed. I was. But I do understand.

I don't take their lack of response as a negative commentary on the book or its intentions. I chalk it up to Justin being a megastar with an untenable number of demands and commitments on his time.

So please don't view the fact that Justin didn't speak to me directly for this book project as a disavowal of his gracious, humble, and, yes, genuine faith. I don't.

As I told Pattie in a letter on that private website, "Please know upfront that, no matter how this ends up going, you have had, have now, and will continue to have my prayerful support for you, your sweet boy, and for his and your mission in the world. You both are a great blessing and testament to God's mercy, faithfulness, and abiding love for all of us."

I meant that sincerely and still do.

The following is my heartfelt prayer for Justin:

When your responsibilities and obligations feel like a burden, and when the concerns of this troubled world weigh you down, may God's joy lift your spirit and may you continue to dance and sing with unfettered joy.

When you feel lonely, like nobody understands, or the voices of the "haterz" are louder than those who love and cheer you on, may you listen for the still, small voice of the One who knows and loves you best and believe what it's saying: "You are my precious, beloved child. Walk on."

When the naysayers say you can't, that it's impossible or that you're not good enough, may you remember that the God who loves you more than anyone else can do anything—ANYTHING—far more than you could imagine in your wildest dreams and that you can do all things through Jesus Christ who strengthens you and lives in your heart.

May you always be a voice for love, grace, hope, and gratitude.

May you always pay it forward and give back and believe.

May you know, deep in your bones, that there is nothing you can do to make God love you more and that there's nothing, not a single thing, you can do to make God love you less.

And may you continue, with boldness and humility, to share the good news of God's love and grace with the world.

Bless you, Justin.

P.S. Hey Justin, if you ever feel like talking about the eternal things that matter most to you, I'm here to listen. You know where to find me.

Conversation Starters

I t is my great hope that this book will be a catalyst for conversations among adults and young people, pastors and their flocks, teachers and students, parents and children, and among friends (old, young, and in between) about the things that matter most in life. Eternal matters such as faith, relationships (with God and other people), how art can reflect and challenge faith, what it means to believe, and how art—music, film, books, television, and even online communities such as Facebook and Twitter—can inspire us to dig deeper into spiritual concerns.

To that end, here are a few questions that might help get the conversation started.

Remember to listen to each other respectfully, to keep confidences safe, and remember that God is in the room with you as you talk to one another.

Be honest and kind.

And pay attention to your lives, especially the things that bring a tear to your eye or put a lump in your throat. No matter what they are (or how unlikely th ey may seem to be), they could be an early warning system that tells you the Holy is getting closer and speaking to your heart.

1. How would you describe yourself spiritually?

2. How does music inspire or move you?

3. What is it about Justin's story or music that appeals to you? Why?

4. Where do you see God's fingerprints in the story of Justin's life?

5. If you could sit down with Justin and talk to him about faith, what would you want to ask him? What would you want to tell him?

6. Have you ever prayed for a celebrity? If so, who? Why? What did you pray for?

7. Have you ever prayed for Justin? If so, why? And what did you pray for?

8. Which of Justin's songs do you find a spiritual connection with and why?

9. Who are other musicians or songs that you connect with spiritually? Why? What does that music mean or say to you?

10. Some people say that Christian believers—or people of faith in general, no matter which spiritual tradition—have no business working in the "secular" entertainment industry. What do you think about that?

11. How do you think God is using Justin to reach the world with the good news?

12. Who are other celebrities you think represent a positive voice for faith in the world?

13. How has Justin's charity work—how he "pays it

forward" or "gives back"—inspired you to get involved in a similar way?

14. What do you do to "pay it forward"? What would you like to get involved with in the future to give back?

15. What films have you seen that you think reflect ideas, good or bad, about faith, God, religion, or spirituality? How do they do so and what is the message they're sending?

16. When you hear Justin or his mother talk about faith or religious issues, what do you take away? What kind of a message do you think they're presenting? Does it inspire you to talk about faith in a different way? If yes, in what way? If no, why not?

17. What kind of a message do you think Justin is sending, in his music or in the way he lives his life publicly, about sexuality?

18. What kinds of things do you hope Justin will write and sing about in his songs in the future?

19. How has the profile of Justin's faith in this book made you think about celebrities and faith in a different way?

20. If you were a celebrity, what would you hope to do or say that would represent what you believe?

#GRATEFUL

As the saying goes, it takes a village . . .

I am especially blessed to have a village peopled by such extraordinarily generous, loving, and supportive friends and family. This book would not have come to fruition without you.

Thank you for Beliebing.

♥ ♥ ♥

David Vanderveen (because this was his idea). Thank you, honey, for being the most generous, loyal, creative, smart, and endlessly entertaining of friends, and for loving me and my family so well.

Chris Ferebee, my intrepid agent and endlessly patient friend

Angela Scheff, my long-suffering, gracious, and ridiculously talented editor

The epic crew (swag!) at Worthy:

Byron Williamson

Rob Birkhead

Sherrie Slopianka

Jeana Ledbetter

Kris Bearss

Dana Long

Morgan Canclini

Dale Wilstermann

David Howell

My two favorite men: Maurice Possley, and my beautiful son, Vasco Fitzmaurice Mark David Possley. You are my home and my fathomless joy.

My amazing parents, Mario and Helen Falsani, and my hero—my not-so-little brother, USAF Captain Mark D. Falsani

The Possley clan:

> Dr. Dan Possley and Dr. Christine Maren (and the player to be named later)
>
> Mike, Britt, Aidan, and McKenna Possley
>
> Tim and Katie Possley
>
> Maura and Casey Cora
>
> Harold and Dorothy Possley
>
> Aunt Rita Sullivan

My chosen family:

> Jennifer Grant and David Funck
>
> Theo, Ian, Maisy, Mimi, and Shiloh Grant-Funck
>
> Kelley, Hannah, and Ethan Ryan
>
> Sissi, Schuyler, and Willem Vanderveen
>
> David, Lisa, Max, and Sam Burchi
>
> Sarah and Cora Metherell
>
> Iris Bourne and Glenn Rogers
>
> Gina, Kate, and Jake Rogers
>
> John Michael, Sara Beth, Anne Elise, Lilly, and Owen "The Colonel" Pillow
>
> Rabbi Allen Secher and Ina Albert
>
> Rabbi Irwin Kula
>
> Keiko and Rob Feldman and Andrew and Zachary Johnson
>
> Jason and Melinda Pearson and their Pearpod
>
> Susan, Briggs, and Max Maynor, and Scott "McFondle" McDonald
>
> Ruth Olsen and Joanna Falk

#Grateful

Mark Hansen

James and Jennifer Johnson

Brian Funck and Sara Hendren and the Funckdrenlings

Carolyn, Sean, Ella, and Sophie Lilly-Wilson

Leeann Drabenstott Culbreath and the Tifton Goobers

Ben, Jen, and precious Nathaniel Mark Greenwald

John Kay On Drums

John and Susan Schmaltzbauer

Jason Harrod, Doug Schauer, James Coder, and Monsignor James Smith

Kathy Ferguson and the Fairy Godmothers

Carolyn and Kairos Reyes

Alex and Pam Metherell

Leila Ehdaie

Jen Bluestein

Cary Shyres and Scott Haug

Trixi, Paul, Kiki, and Teague Hamilton

Tania, Steve, Tyler, and Tatum Cassill

Knute, Nikki, Kiana, and Cameron Keeling

My Little Church family:

Jeff and Patty Tacklind

Brad and Margie Coleman

Clarke and Annie Brogger

Jay and Nikki Grant

Mary Hurlbutt

Vicki High

The Arthurs

Jeff LeFever

Dave and Dallas Day

Kim Day

Katie, Joel, Leah, Ava, and Emmett Vanderveen

Dave and Ali Tosti

The Radach Family

My beautiful global village of gracious souls:

Deborah Abramson, who, from the other side of the country, volunteered to transcribe Belieber interviews in the middle of the night—amazing grace, you!

Adam Phillips

Jack Heaslip

Bono

Kathy McKiernan

Luisa Engel

The Edge, Adam Clayton, Larry Mullen Jr., and Paul McGuinness

Catriona Garde and Susan Hunter

Riley and Lisa Page

Frankie Page

Margaret Feinberg

Rob Bell

St. Freddie of Rupert

Dan Adler

Sara Tucker

The Herrick Family

Naomi Duncan, Dana Ashley, and the folks at Ambassador

Tripp Hudgins

Kevin Eckstrom

Tim Townsend

Jim Wallis

Michael Cooke

Caroline Galloway

#Grateful

Camille Birkhead and the NashVegas Beliebers

Beth Hood

Tammy Faxel and Wayne Shepherd at Oasis Audio

Annie Weiland

Chris Smit

Sam Phillips and Bruce Cockburn

Lynda Gorov

The Luft Family

The Nordlof Family

Patricia and Carly McTague

Bridget Nugent

Yaphet Tedla and The Wheaton Beliebers

Magdalena Schreck

Todd Yates

The folks at EMI for getting me a ticket to the Billboard Awards

Mark Rodgers

Tina Simpkin

A very special thanks to Justin, Pattie, Scooter, Mama Jan, Kenny, Ryan, Alison, Bruce, Diane, Jeremy, Usher, and L.A. for your part in helping to share Justin's incredible story with the world.

May you continue to bless and be blessed. Thank you for paying it forward with so much grace.

And, as always, to Linda Richardson, for giving me wings . . .

Notes

Chapter 1: Beliebing

13: *"Whenever you knock me down"*: Justin Bieber, Adam Messinger, Jaden Smith, et al., "Never Say Never," theme song from *The Karate Kid* (2010).

Chapter 2: In the Beginning

20: *"Freaks [him] out"*: Justin Bieber, *First Step 2 Forever: My Story* (New York: HarperCollins, 2010), 31.

20: *"Pattie and Jeremy were engaged"*: Pattie Mallette quoted in "Justin Bieber: My World," *E! News Special*, July 2010.

20: *"When Justin's dad"*: Mallette quoted in "Justin Bieber: My World," *E! News Special*.

20: *"My dad was away"*: Bieber, *First Step 2 Forever*, 40.

21: *"When he was a baby"*: Mallette quoted in "Justin Bieber: My World," *E! News Special*.

21: *"Our extended family"*: Bieber, *First Step 2 Forever*, 35.

23: *"For all of his life"*: Bieber, *First Step 2 Forever*, 23.

24: *Butler*: Martin Butler quoted in *Never Say Never*, directed by Jon M. Chu (MTV Films/Scooter Braun Films), 2011.

24: *"I depend"*: Bieber, *First Step 2 Forever*, 182.

24: *"I have an amazing"*: Pattie Mallette interviewed in "Running from Pain and Finding Hope," *100 Huntley*, June 2008, http://www.100huntley.com/video .php?id=dMp08SVsQnM.

25: *"I told him"*: Mallette quoted in Phil Boatwright, "Justin Bieber's mom opens up about faith, spotlight," *Baptist Press*, February 9, 2011, http://www .bpnews.net/BPFirstPerson.asp?ID=34625.

26: *Bootsma*: John Bootsma quoted in "Faith Behind the Fame: The Prayers of Justin Bieber's Mother," *100 Huntley*, March 28, 2011, www.100huntley.com/video.php?id=_8T0FaBmJd0.

26: *McKay*: Nathan McKay quoted in *Never Say Never*.

27: *"Pattie's friends"*: "Justin Bieber: My World," *E! News Special*.

27: *"And he was good"*: Bruce Dale quoted in "Justin Bieber: My World," *E! News Special*.

28: *"Those harmonies"*: Bieber, *First Step 2 Forever*, 56.

29: *"In the Bible"*: Bieber, *First Step 2 Forever*.

Chapter 3: The Fairy Godmanager

42: *"He called"*: Justin Bieber interviewed by Nicholas Kohler, "McLeans Interview: Justin Bieber," *McLeans Magazine*, December 19, 2009, http://www2.macleans.ca/2009/12/15/macleans-interview-justin-bieber.

43: *"Please, listen"*: Scooter Braun quoted in Justin Bieber, *First Step 2 Forever: My Story* (New York: HarperCollins, 2010), 110.

44: *"I prayed"*: Pattie Mallette quoted in Jan Hoffman, "Justin Bieber Is Living the Dream," *New York Times*, December 31, 2009, http://www.nytimes.com/2010/01/03/fashion/03bieber.html?pagewanted=all.

44: *"I got her talking"*: Scooter Braun quoted in Larry LeBlanc, "Industry Profile: Scooter Braun," *Celebrity Access Event Wire*, February 2011, http://www.celebrityaccess.com/members/profile.html?id=546.

47: *"He was so good"*: Coley Ward, "Scooter Braun is the Hustla," *Creative Loafing Atlanta*, May 10, 2006, http://clatl.com/atlanta/the-hustla/Content?oid=1258376.

47: *"By the end"*: LeBlanc, "Industry Profile: Scooter Braun."

47: *"I thought"*: Braun quoted in LeBlanc, "Industry Profile: Scooter Braun."

48: *"I definitely got"*: Braun quoted in LeBlanc, "Industry Profile: Scooter Braun."

48: *"At the beginning"*: Braun quoted in LeBlanc, "Industry Profile: Scooter Braun."

48: *"Justin's reaction"*: Bieber, *First Step 2 Forever*, 115.

49: *"Asher's debut"*: LeBlanc, "Industry Profile: Scooter Braun."

52: *"Within a month"*: Bieber, *First Step 2 Forever*, 124-25.

52: *"Nothing great"*: Braun quoted in Bieber, *First Step 2 Forever*, 126.

54: *"We said goodbye"*: Bieber, *First Step 2 Forever*, 154.

Chapter 4: A Wing of Protection

56: *"It was just"*: Pattie Mallette interviewed in "Running from Pain and Finding Hope," *100 Huntley*, June 2008, http://www.100huntley.com/video.php?id=dMp08SVsQnM. Unless otherwise noted, all quotes from Pattie Mallette in this chapter are taken from her 2008 interview with the *100 Huntley* program.

58: *Thompson*: Francis Thompson, "Hound of Heaven," 1909.

63: *Bootsma*: John Bootsma interviewed in "Faith Behind the Fame: The Prayers of Justin Bieber's Mother," *100 Huntley*, March 28, 2011, www.100huntley.com/video.php?id=_8T0FaBmJd0.

Chapter 5: Praying It Forward

66: *"God is strong"*: Ephesians 6:11-18.

67: *"Go between for God"*: Some believers call this "standing in the gap," an expression that comes from the Hebrew Scriptures: "I looked for someone to stand up for me against all this, to repair the defenses of the city, to take a stand for me and stand in the gap to protect this land so I wouldn't have to destroy it. I couldn't find anyone. Not one" (Ezekiel 22:30).

68: *Kierkegaard:* Søren Kierkegaard, *Purity of Heart: Is to Will One Thing* (New York: Harper & Row, 1938), 25.

68: *"Absolutely everything":* Matthew 21:21-22.

68: *"As a woman":* Pattie Mallette in the foreword for *Never Say Never: For Nothing Is Impossible with God* (Allied Faith & Family/Allied Media, 2011), 1.

68: *James 5:16:* "Make this your common practice: Confess your sins to each other and pray for each other so that you can live together whole and healed. The prayer of a person living right with God is something powerful to be reckoned with."

69: *"Justin is 17":* "Prayer for Justin Bieber," Hollywood Prayer Network, January 2011, http://www.hollywoodprayernetwork.org/content/prayer-justin-bieber.

71: *"We are very selective":* Pattie Mallette in an interview with Hollywood Prayer Network, uploaded March 2, 2011, http://youtube/N8IdkanPG2E.

72: *"I do have peace":* Pattie Mallette in an interview with Hollywood Prayer Network, uploaded February 15, 2011, http://youtube/Q0c0bzDRigE.

75: *"He's trying":* Pattie Mallette quoted in Tim Townsend, "Documentary connects the dots between Bieber, Christian audience," *St. Louis Post-Dispatch,* February 20, 2011, 8B.

76: *"I know":* Mallette quoted in Townsend, "Documentary connects the dots between Bieber, Christian audience."

76: *"I'm aware":* Pattie Mallette quote in Kate Shellnut, "Believe it or not, Justin Bieber sticks to his faith despite fame," *Houston Chronicle,* February 4, 2011, 2.

76: *"It's been":* Pattie Mallette in an interview with Hollywood Prayer Network, uploaded April 15, 2011, http://youtube/6HQLYHbMFps.

Chapter 6: His World

85: *Bieber:* Justin Bieber, Adam Messinger, "Up," *My World 2.0* (Island Def Jam), 2010.

86: *"One day":* Story recounted in "Justin Bieber: My World," *E! News Special,* July 2010.

86: *Roth:* Asher Roth quoted in Justin Bieber, *First Step 2 Forever: My Story* (New York: HarperCollins, 2010), 150.

87: *"I don't care":* Pattie Mallette quoted in Bieber, *First Step 2 Forever.*

88: *Usher:* Usher quoted in Bieber, *First Step 2 Forever.*

90: *"When broken hearts":* Justin Bieber, Lashaunda Carr, "Common Denominator" [Bonus Track], *My World* EP (Island Records), 2009.

92: *Usher:* Usher quoted in "Justin Bieber: My World," *E! News Special.*

94: *"If he isn't":* Kenny Hamilton quoted in "Justin Bieber: My World," *E! News Special.*

94: *Mama Jan:* Quoted in "Justin Bieber: My World," *E! News Special.*

95: *"Most of the young":* Mallette quoted in "Justin Bieber: My World," *E! News Special.*

95: *"One time":* Bieber quoted in "Justin Bieber: My World," *E! News Special.*

95: *"Everyone is waiting":* Scooter Braun quoted in Chris Hodenfield, "Brains & Braun," *Greenwich Magazine,* December 2010.

96: *"It's his biggest struggle":* Braun quoted in Larry LeBlanc, "Industry Profile: Scooter Braun," *Celebrity Access Event Wire,* February 2011, http://www. celebrityaccess.com/members/profile.html?id=546.

96: *"There's a great":* Usher quoted in "Justin Bieber: My World," *E! News Special.*

Chapter 8: #killemwithkindness

112: *"There are always":* Justin Bieber in a video interview with Jake Hamilton, *Jake's Takes,* February 2011, http://youtu.be/CVby86nqNCE.

Chapter 9: Nobody's Perfect

119: *"He's so":* Pattie Mallette in an interview with "Today Moms," *The Today Show,* NBC, 2009, http://youtu.be/C58hwuR-jFE.

120: *"It's definitely":* Justin Bieber in an interview with New Zealand television, May 2011. http://youtu.be/Tv0HAKgYpLY

121: *"There's going":* Scooter Braun quoted by Piet Levy, "Tween Evangelist? Justin Bieber film packed with prayer," *USA Today,* Feb. 2, 2011, http://www .usatoday.com/news/religion/2011-02-10-Justin_Bieber_evangelical_08_ ST_N.htm.

122: *Poll:* Reuters, "Justin Bieber will be headed for celebrity rehab by age 30, says poll," *The New York Daily News,* March 29, 2011, http://articles.nydaily-news.com/2011-03-29/gossip/29378441_1_justin-bieber-celebrity -rehab-squeaky-clean-pop-star.

Chapter 10: Voice of a Generation

131: *Grigoriadis:* Vanessa Grigoriadis, "Justin Bieber: Super Boy," *Rolling Stone,* February 2011.

138: *"I think":* Justin Bieber in an interview with *60 Minutes Australia,* April 2011.

Chapter 11: Tikkun Olam

161: *"My mother said":* Scooter Braun quoted in Larry LeBlanc, "Industry Profile: Scooter Braun," *Celebrity Access Event Wire,* February 2011, http://www .celebrityaccess.com/members/profile.html?id=546.

162: *"My mom":* Scooter Braun quoted in Chris Hodenfield, "Brains & Braun," *Greenwich Magazine,* December 2010.

162: *"My parents"*: Braun quoted in "Managing Justin Bieber," AISH.com, February 2011, http://www.aish.com/j/as/Managing_Justin_Bieber.html.

163: *"A kingdom of priests"*: Exodus 19:5-6.

163: *"A light for the nations"*: Isaiah 49:6.

163: *"You're here"*: Matthew 5:13-14.

165: *"His mother spent"*: "Managing Justin Bieber," AISH.com.

165: *"They eventually"*: Hodenfield, "Brains & Braun."

165: *"Ervin's father"*: LeBlanc, "Industry Profile: Scooter Braun."

165: *"So Ervin"*: Naomi Pfefferman, "Justin Bieber's Jewish Father Figure, Scooter Braun," *The Jewish Journal*, February 8, 2011, http://www.jewishjournal. com/the_ticket/item/my_interview_with_scooter_braun_justin_biebers_ jewish_father_figure_2011020/.

166: *"There was no"*: Ervin Braun quoted in Pfefferman, "Justin Bieber's Jewish Father Figure, Scooter Braun."

166: *"As a kid"*: Hodenfield, "Brains & Braun."

166: *"My heroes"*: Scooter Braun quoted in Hodenfield, "Brains & Braun."

167: *"She gave Scooter"*: Bieber, *First Step 2 Forever: My Story* (New York: Harper-Collins, 2010), 121-22.

167: *"The brothers"*: "Managing Justin Bieber," AISH.com.

167: *"I think"*: Braun as quoted in Hodenfield, "Brains & Braun."

167: *"People always"*: Braun quoted in LeBlanc, "Industry Profile: Scooter Braun."

168: *"Justin is"*: Braun quoted in LeBlanc, "Industry Profile: Scooter Braun."

168: *"I'm not going"*: Braun quoted in Pfefferman, "Justin Bieber's Jewish Father Figure, Scooter Braun."

169: *"If you treat"*: Braun quoted in "Managing Justin Bieber," AISH.com.

170: *"I think"*: Braun quoted in Dan Schawbel, "Inside the Brand of Justin Bieber: An Interview with Manager Scooter Page: Braun," *Forbes*, February 11, 2011, http://blogs.forbes.com/danschawbel/2011/02/11/inside-the-brand-of-justin-bieber-an-interview-with-manager-scooter-braun/.

171: *"They have been"*: Dan Kanter quoted in Naomi Pfefferman, "Justin Bieber's Musical Father Figure, Dan Kanter," *Jewish Journal*, May 18, 2011, http://www.jewishjournal.com/the_ticket/item/justin_biebers_musical_ father_figure_dan_kanter_20110518/.

172: *"I felt like"*: Braun quoted in Pfefferman, "Justin Bieber's Jewish Father Figure, Scooter Braun."

173: *Miller*: Jason Miller, "Justin Bieber Says the Shema & Other Jewish Customs Adopted by Non-Jews," Rabbi Jason blog, October 5, 2010, http://blog .rabbijason.com/2010/10/justin-bieber-says-shema-other-jewish.html.

173: *"Justin has"*: Braun quoted in "Managing Justin Bieber," AISH.com.

Notes

227

Chapter 12: Pay It Forward

175: *Bono:* Bono, interviewed by Cathleen Falsani, December 2002. Quote also appeared in Falsani's article, "Bono's American Prayer," *Christianity Today,* March 2003, http://www.christianitytoday.com/ct/2003/march/2.38.html.

176: *"Watched as a wave":* Adam Braun, "Our Story," Pencils of Promise, http://www.pencilsofpromise.org/who-we-are/our-story.

176: *"I'd come home":* Adam Braun quoted in Jenny Inglee, "The Right to Write: How One Pencil Started a Revolution," TakePart.org, Feb. 24, 2011, http://www.takepart.com/news/2011/02/24/pencils-of-promise.

177: *"My grandfathers":* Adam Braun quoted in Inglee, "The Right to Write."

177: *"In October":* Lisa Chamoff, "Something to 'Belieb' In," *Connecticut Post,* July 3, 2011.

177: *"An estimated":* That kind of phenomenon is why global basic education is second on the United Nation's list of "Millennium Development Goals," eight goals that all 192 UN member nations have agreed to work toward achieving by the year 2015.

178: *"By the time":* "Schools 4 All: A Special Message to Our Supporters," Pencils of Promise, July 1, 2011, http://www.pencilsofpromise.org/blog/the-pop-movement/schools4all-a-special-message-to-our-supporters.

178: *"Justin is":* Adam Braun quoted in Inglee, "The Right to Write."

179: *"I just think":* Justin Beiber interviewed in Alina Cho, *Big Stars, Big Giving,* CNN, December 25, 2010.

179: *"It's really easy":* Bieber interviewed in Cho, *Big Stars, Big Giving.*

180: *Mayer:* John Mayer, "Waiting on the World to Change," *Continuum* (Aware/Columbia), 2006.

181: *"I didn't have":* Bieber interviewed in Cho, *Big Stars, Big Giving.*

181: *I am in":* Bieber quoted in "Fresh off the AMA's: Artist of the Year Justin Bieber Donating Portion of Proceeds of New Album to Children's Miracle Network," *Business Wire,* Nov. 24, 2010, http://www.businesswire.com/news/home/20101124005933/en/Fresh-AMAs-Artist-Year-Justin-Bieber-Donating.

181: *"They flew":* Bieber interviewed in Cho, *Big Stars, Big Giving.*

183: *"My dad":* Bieber quoted on PETA's website, September 2009, http://www.peta2.com/outthere/o-justinbieber.asp?c=p23743.

184: *"A month after":* Catherine Balavage, "Justin Bieber's Perfume Rakes in Over 3 Million," *Frost,* July 17, 2011, http://frostmagazine.com/2011/07/justin-biebers-perfume-rakes-in-over-3-million/.

184: *Haugen:* Brad Haugen quoted in Lisa Chamoff, "Something to 'Belieb' In," *Connecticut Post,* July 3, 2011.

Chapter 13: #BELIEVE

203: *"I meant to tell you"*: In early 2011, a song called "Believe," that has not appeared on any of Justin's albums to date, leaked online. It's not clear whether this was a new recording or something left over from previous recording sessions for his first albums. The audio recordings were briefly uploaded to a number of Internet sites but have since been taken down because of alleged copyright violations. The lyrics, however, remain listed on a number of websites. See http://www.songonlyrics.com/justin-bieber -believe-lyrics.

203: *"To think"*: Justin Bieber as quoted in Shirley Halperin, "Justin Bieber: 'With Time Off I'm Able to Think, Pray and Grow Up' (Exclusive)," Hollywood Reporter, July 20, 2011, http://www.hollywoodreporter.com/news/justin -bieber-time-im-think-213063.

205: *"Justin's father"*: "Meet Jeremy Jack Bieber," InfoStar Celebrity Blog, April 15, 2011, http://infostarcelebrity.blogspot.com/2011/04/meet-jeremy-jack -bieber-justins.html.

206: *"Rounding out"*: Troy Rogers, "Justin Bieber Has Most Viewed Internet Video," TheDeadbolt.com, July 3, 2011, http://www.thedeadbolt.com/ news/1000548/justin_bieber_most_viewed_internet_video.php.

207: *"I want"*: Bieber quoted by Perez Hilton, "Justin Bieber talks new album!" *PerezHilton.com*, June 29, 2011, http://perezhilton.com/2011-06-29-justin -bieber-talks-new-album.

208: *"Justin is"*: Dan Kanter quoted in Pfefferman, "Justin Bieber's Musical Father Figure, Dan Kanter," *The Jewish Journal*, May 18, 2011, http://www. jewishjournal.com/the_ticket/item/justin_biebers_musical_father_figure_ dan_kanter_20110518/.

209: *"In a move"*: "Daniel Lanois to Produce Justin Bieber's New Album in July 2011," JustinBieberZone.com, April 1, 2011, http://www.justinbieberzone .com/2011/04/daniel-lanois-to-produce-justin-biebers-new-album-in -july-2011.

210: *"Hollywood"*: Chris Hodenfield, "Brains & Braun," *Greenwich Magazine*, December 2010.

210: *"Scooter has"*: Larry LeBlanc, "Industry Profile: Scooter Braun," *Celebrity Access Event Wire*, February 2011, http://www.celebrityaccess.com/ members/profile.html?id=546.

211: *"I want"*: Just Bieber quoted by Tom Ayres, "Bieber: 'I want to go to university,'" Digital Spy, Nov. 20, 2010, http://www.digitalspy.com/celebrity/news/ a290608/bieber-i-want-to-go-to-university.html

Cathleen Falsani is an award-winning religion journalist and author who specializes in the intersection of spirituality and popular culture. Currently a columnist for Religion News Service and an editor for *Sojourners* in Washington, D.C., Cathleen is best known for her personal interview profiles of Barack Obama, Bono of U2, Elie Wiesel, Anne Rice, Studs Terkel, Annie Lennox and many other notables. She is the author of three critically acclaimed books: *The God Factor, Sin Boldly* and *The Dude Abides: The Gospel According to the Coen Brothers*. Religion writer for the *Chicago Sun-Times* from 2000-2010, Cathleen now lives in Laguna Beach, California, with her husband, fellow author and Pulitzer Prize-winning journalist Maurice Possley, and their son, Vasco.

WORTHY

P U B L I S H I N G

IF YOU LIKED THIS BOOK . . .

- Tell your friends by going to: http://justin-book.com and clicking "LIKE"
- Share the video book trailer by posting it on your Facebook page
- Head over to our Facebook page, click "LIKE" and post a comment regarding what you enjoyed about the book
- Tweet "I recommend reading @BeliebertheBook by @godgrrl @Worthypub"
- Hashtag: #BeliebertheBook
- Subscribe to our newsletter by going to http://worthypublishing.com/about/subscribe.php

WORTHY PUBLISHING
FACEBOOK PAGE

WORTHY PUBLISHING
WEBSITE